The Freemasons
in America

The Freemasons in America

Inside the Secret Society

H. PAUL JEFFERS

CITADEL PRESS
Kensington Publishing Corp.
www.kensingtonbooks.com

CITADEL PRESS BOOKS are published by

Kensington Publishing Corp.
850 Third Avenue
New York, NY 10022

All Kensington titles, imprints, and distributed lines are available at special
quantity discounts for bulk purchases for sales promotions, premiums, fund-
raising, educational, or institutional use. Special book excerpts or customized
printings can also be created to fit specific needs. For details, write or phone the
office of the Kensington special sales manager: Kensington Publishing Corp.,
850 Third Avenue, New York, NY 10022, attn: Special Sales Department;
phone 1-800-221-2647.

CITADEL PRESS and the Citadel logo are Reg. U.S. Pat. & TM Off.

First trade paperback printing: September 2007

10 9 8 7 6 5 4 3 2 1

Printed in the United States of America

Library of Congress Control Number: 2006926715

ISBN-13: 978-0-8065-2836-6
ISBN-10: 0-8065-2836-2

In Memoriam

PETER JENNINGS

colleague and friend, ABC News, 1965–68

I enjoy going to some little lodge where I meet the plain hard-working people on the basis of genuine equality. It is the equality of moral men.
—Theodore Roosevelt

Contents

Introduction: Codes, Secrets, and Mysterious Masons

Knights Templar!
Freemasons!
Skullduggery and cover-up by the Roman Catholic Church!

So fascinating, fantastic, and fabulous are the mystique and mystery surrounding the world's oldest secret society and the medieval Crusader knights that it is easy to accept fiction and myth as fact. Millions of people around the globe found credibility in the novel *The Da Vinci Code* by Dan Brown with its theme that the Knights Templar and the church were at the core of a thousand-year conspiracy to suppress documentary proof that Jesus had wed Mary Magdalene, that she ranked first among the apostles, and that at the time of his crucifixion she was carrying his child. Following the birth of a daughter named Sarah, Mary fled Jerusalem and took the baby to Egypt. Twelve years later, they settled in the Roman province of Gaul (present-day southern France). When written evidence of this was discovered in Jerusalem by the Templars during the Crusades, the church suppressed knowledge of the evidence to sustain its authority in the Christian world. If all this were true, descendants of Christ are among us today and may be living in Europe and possibly the United States.

It is historical fact that a small army of French knights set out to liberate the Holy City of Jerusalem from Muslims and set up headquarters near the Temple Mount, the site of the Hebrews' first temple. Built by King Solomon and destroyed by invading Babylonians, and then rebuilt by Herod the Great, it was the Temple in the time of Jesus. As protectors of the sacred ground that had been wrenched from Muslims, the knights became known as the Templars. In Brown's book and in earlier treatments of the history of the Templars, including the nonfiction *Holy Blood, Holy Grail* by Michael Baigent and Richard Leigh, also authors of *The Temple and the Lodge,* they discovered evidence of Jesus's marriage to Magdalene and became keepers and protectors of the secret. In medieval tradition and the mythology of the Middle Ages, such as King Arthur and the knights of Camelot, the only surviving artifact of Jesus's last supper was the cup he used to share wine with the thirteen apostles, including Judas Iscariot. This chalice became known as the Holy Grail because it signified the blood of Christ. In *Holy Blood, Holy Grail* and *The Da Vinci Code,* the Grail is not a cup, but Jesus's daughter. According to Brown's novel, the proof that Magdalene was Jesus's closest apostle was encoded in Leonardo da Vinci's fresco painting *The Last Supper.* The Knights Templar as a financial and political power in Europe came to an abrupt end when the order was crushed and its leadership executed by France's King Philip IV with the connivance of Pope Clement V.

A film released in 2004 called *National Treasure* thrust Freemasonry into the history of the founding of the United States. It presented a story about a huge treasure of priceless loot accumulated by the Templars during and after the Crusades. These riches were eventually taken to the British colonies in America and hidden during the Revolutionary War by Founding Fathers who were Masons, including Benjamin Franklin. Clues to the location of this treasure trove were concealed in national landmarks and historical documents of the United States.

Being a writer of history and a few mystery and detective novels, but with almost total ignorance on the topic of Freemasonry, I became intrigued by the tidal wave of popular interest in the Masons that these fictional phenomena unleashed. The result of my quest for knowledge on the topic resulted in my book *Freemasonry: Inside the World's Oldest Secret Society.* I learned that the Masons are an international fraternity, although some lodges admit women. Membership is open to adults who believe in a "Supreme Divine Being" and the immortality of the soul. While Freemasonry does not claim to be a religion, its beliefs are influenced by eighteenth- and nineteenth-century universalism and deism.

Critics find in it influences of occultism, anti-Christianity, and even Satanism. The Vatican has banned Catholics from becoming Freemasons since the sixteenth century. While Masons are found all over the world, the fraternal society is not a monolithic organization with a central authority figure, such as a pope, international president, secretary-general, board of directors, or other overarching global executive. The governing body in a country is the "grand lodge." In the United States, there is one for each state in which Masonry exists, but no national body. There are more Freemasons in the United States than anywhere in the world.

Members engage in rituals and rites that are said to date to the building of King Solomon's Temple. Common ancient tools used in construction are employed symbolically in ceremonies. The trowel, plumb, level, and compass are related to building character and morality and the advancement of the members to the understanding of the "Universal Light." The tools are at the center of a lodge meeting, along with a Bible, the Koran in Muslim areas of the world, or any book sacred to other religions. Also required to be displayed is the letter G. It stands for the "Great Architect of the Universe" (God). Although Freemasons are sworn to secrecy concerning what they call the Craft and because they pledge unquestioning loyalty to each other, the popular belief is that Freemasonry is a sinister organization that controls the United States and is trying to establish a "New World Order."

Freemasons answer that they are idealists who study and celebrate common moral beliefs and individual improvement and perform charitable works. A man seeking membership begins as "entered apprentice" and by study moves up to "fellowcraft" and "grand master." These stages are called "degrees." A "lodge" is both the membership and the building where they meet. Because ceilings of American meeting halls are painted blue to represent the heavens, U.S. Freemasonry is known as "Blue Lodge." A meeting place of Masonry named "York Rite" is a "temple." Origins of the fraternity are debated by Masons themselves. Some accounts trace it back to the murder of the architect of King Solomon's Temple, Hiram Abiff, who was killed by three apprentices who resented not being granted the title grand master, earlier accounts to

Greece and Egypt, and to the men of the Middle Ages who built Gothic cathedrals. The style was intended to lift the devotion of the masses by using soaring lines and ascending curves in a graceful design to glorify God. In Britain, these men were categorized by those who handled hard stone ("hard hewers" or "rough masons") and more highly skilled cutters of softer, chalky rock (known as "free stone"). Because these artisans were free to travel and set their own wage scale, they were called "free stonemasons." This was eventually shortened to "freemasons." By 1292, English masons called a hut near their worksite where they stored tools and had meals a "lodge."

What is certain about modern Freemasonry is that in Britain in 1717 several small lodges formed the United Grand Lodge of England as a governing body. As the British Empire extended to America, Freemasonry followed, initially in military lodges. Many of the Founding Fathers were Freemasons. Masonic historians contend that it was at the heart of the American struggle for independence and became the cornerstone of the structure of the U.S. government.

In exploring these aspects as the primary purpose of this book, invaluable sources were found in the work of Masonic scholars and "research" lodges, which have shared their findings with brother Masons and the public in articles and on many lodge home page Web sites. Without their diligent work, completing this book would have been made considerably more challenging. Where possible, their work is noted in the text, and it is gratefully acknowledged here. Enlightening data was also found in numerous books listed in the Further Reading section.

Summaries of material covered in my previous look at Freemasonry's general history and its rites and rituals are provided where needed to furnish background and a broad context to explain Freemasonry's evolution in the United States. This book necessarily duplicates some material covered in *Freemasons* on the role of the Masonic brotherhood in helping to foment the Revolutionary War and other conflicts, the writing of fundamental national documents, and the role and significance of Freemasonry throughout the political and social history of the United States. The overall story and characteristics of the brotherhood in Britian and Europe are covered in my previous book and by other writers. At the end of this volume are answers to frequently asked questions about Freemasonry. Rites, rituals, and degrees of Freemasonry are provided in the text only to the extent required to illuminate Masonry's controversial and very colorful participation in many aspects of American history.

Because this book deals with questions of credibility in the history of Freemasonry, I note for the record that I am not and never have been a Mason.

The Freemasons
in America

Chapter 1

Godfather: Lord Jeffrey Amherst and American Military Masonry

Lord Jeffrey Amherst was a soldier of the king
And he came from across the sea;
To the Frenchmen and the Indians he didn't do a thing
In the wilds of this wild country,
But for his Royal Majesty he fought with all his might
For he was a soldier brave and true;
He conquered all his enemies whenever they came in sight
And he looked around for more when he was through.

WHEN STUDENTS AND FACULTY OF AMHERST COLLEGE IN MASSA-chusetts join in their school's song, it is a tribute to its name-sake, a British army officer who arrived in America to command soldiers in a world war with France. Born in Riverhead, Seven-oaks, England, he was the son of another Jeffery Amherst, a prosperous lawyer whose family had lived in Kent for centuries. At the age of twelve, young Jeffery became a page in the house of Lionel Cranfield Sackville, the First Duke of Dorset. Circumstances of his early military career are obscure. It has been noted that he entered the First Foot Guards as an en-sign. A list of officers in the regimental history shows him doing so in November 1735. Made a lieutenant in Sir John Ligonier's Regiment of Horse, which was based in Ireland, he became a protégé of Ligonier, who called him his "dear pupil."

Amherst saw his first active service as Ligonier's aide-de-camp in Germany during the War of the Austrian Succession and was present at

1

the battles of Dettingen in Germany in 1743 and Fontenoy (Belgium) in 1745. The First Foot Guards' records show that in December 1745 he was appointed captain in that regiment, a commission carrying with it the rank of lieutenant-colonel in the army at large. In 1747, the Duke of Cumberland, as commander in chief of the allied forces in Europe, made him one of his aides-de-camp. He served during the Battle of Laffeldt (Belgium).

In a period of peace following the Treaty of Aix-la-Chapelle (1748), he was in England. His first responsibility in the Seven Years' War with France was as "commissary" in charge of the administration of 8,000 Hessian troops taken into British pay at the beginning of 1756. He went to Germany in February to undertake a duty that seems to have been largely financial. He returned to England in May with part of the Hessian force to guard against a possible invasion by the French. Soon after his return, he was appointed colonel of the Fifteenth Foot. This commission did not involve active command of the regiment, so he returned to Germany with the Hessian detachment in March 1757. He was at the victorious battle of Hastenbeck on July 26, 1757. In October, Ligonier succeeded as commander in chief with command of the army in Great Britain and direction over all British troops serving in North America.

After deciding on an assault on Louisbourg Île Royale (Cape Breton Island), in French Canada in 1757, Ligonier placed Amherst in command. This was remarkable, not merely because Amherst was very junior in the army, but because he had never commanded troops in action. With a royal sanction for the grant of the local rank of "Major General in America," Amherst sailed for America on March 16, 1758, with detailed orders for the expedition against Louisbourg. When the British fleet of warships and transports met Amherst just outside the harbor at Gabarus Bay, west of Louisbourg, Amherst studied the shoreline with two brigadiers. He chose to attack from the east. After his force landed, he made a systematic European-style siege operation against the town. The French surrendered.

Leaving a garrison at Louisbourg, Amherst sailed for Boston. When its grateful citizens attempted to get his men drunk, he withdrew his five battalions and marched north to Albany. Because of an earlier British defeat in that region, he discovered that the Louisbourg victory had made him commander in chief in America. He went to New York, where he spent the winter making plans and logistic arrangements for the campaign of 1759, which included another attack on Canada based on orders from London stating that it was "the great and essential object." He was told that "according as you shall, from your knowledge of the Countries, thro' which the War is to be carried, and from emergent circumstances not to be known here, judge the same to be most expedient." He discerned that the French defenders of Montreal were vulnerable because the Canadian militia had largely deserted and the defenders had shrunk to little more than 2,000 men. The British forces amounted to 17,000. Rather than surrender their colors, the French battalions burned them. Montreal, and with it Canada, was surrendered to him on September 8, 1760. Although the fighting with France in North America was virtually over, the war was not.

As commander in chief, Amherst was concerned with organizing expeditions against Dominica and Martinique in 1761. In 1762, he sent a contingent to take part in an attack on the city of Havana, Cuba. In August 1762, he dispatched his younger brother, William, with a hastily assembled force to take St. John's, Newfoundland. In 1763, when word of peace in Europe arrived, Amherst received reports from the west of Indian attacks. They were the opening shots of an uprising by Indians under Chief Pontiac, aided by the French, that was soon named the French and Indian War. Amherst wrote to Sir William Johnson in London, "When Men of What race soever, behave ill they must be punished."

Wherever the British army went, Freemasonry accompanied it in the form of regimental filed lodges. They were mobile and carried their Masonic regalia in trunks along with their regimental colors, silver, and other purely military equipment. In *The Temple and the Lodge,* Michael Baigent and Richard Leigh note that often the colonel commanding would preside as the lodge's original master and then be succeeded by other officers. These regimental field lodges were to have a profound effect on the army as a whole and on Americans who fought beside their homeland cousins.

The first British army lodge was the First Foot Guards to which Amherst was assigned as an aide-de-camp for General Ligonier. Although his full Masonic history is not known, the single most important British commander of the period was a known Mason as early as 1732. At that time there were five regimental lodges, including the Royal Scot Fusiliers, the Gloucester Regiment, the Duke of Wellington's Fusiliers, and the Royal Northumberland Fusiliers, best known to the readers of Sherlock Holmes stories as the regiment in which Dr. John H. Watson served and was wounded in Britain's second war in Afghanistan.

Americans who served British contingents and received military training and instructions in strategy and tactics were also introduced to the rites and rituals of a branch of Freemasonry that was not charted by the Grand Lodge of England, but by the Irish Grand Lodge. The York Rite offered higher degrees (up to thirty-two) and other recognitions of Masonic achievement. The civilian rite that would flourish in the United States was called "Scottish," despite the fact that it was formed in France by English expatriates and had made its way to the American continent through the West Indies.

In a speech titled "American Masonic Roots in British Military Lodges," James R. Case, a master in the American Lodge of Research in New York City, explained that the existence and broad popularity of military Freemasonry resulted from British troops being garrisoned in winter, "For obvious reasons when the army is in the field, there is no opportunity for work or festivity by the Craft."

Although Amherst brought military Freemasonry to the colonies, he was not the first English Mason to set foot on American soil. The pioneer was John Skene. Born in Newtyle, England, around 1649, he, his family, and other daring venturers into the New World sailed up the Delaware River aboard the *Golden Lion* in 1682. Settling at Mount Holly, New Jersey, on a plantation that he named Peachland, he went on to become the deputy colonial governor of West Jersey. He died in 1690. The first Freemason born in America, Andrew Belcher, was the son of

Jonathan Belcher, a former governor of Massachusetts and New Hampshire who had been made a Mason in 1704. Andrew was admitted in 1733. Three years earlier (June 1730), the Grand Master of England had appointed Daniel Coxe of New Jersey to be the first Grand Master of the New World, but Coxe was apparently not much interested in vigorously promoting the brotherhood in the colonies. Under "General History of Freemasonry" in the authoritative *Dictionary of Freemasonry* by Robert Macoy, it is stated that if "Bro. Coxe exercised any of the powers delegated to him we are not informed, nor has any evidence of action on his part been discovered." The entry also recorded, "The first authentic information that we have is that a convention of Masons in the State was held at the city of New Brunswick, December 18, 1786."

By that year, Americans who had learned about Freemasonry and how to fight a war from Amherst had been free of British rule for ten years and at peace for three. After more than five years in North America, Amherst had returned to England and wrote a friend, "I may tell you for your own information only, that I have no thought of returning to America." Historians of his role in the French and Indian War assign him the questionable distinction of being the first to conduct biological warfare. In a series of letters to Colonel Henry Bouquet, a subordinate, he discussed the possibility of sending gifts of blankets infected with smallpox to the Indians. What they did not know was that the commander of Fort Pitt had already attempted the brutal tactic. Because Amherst was the overall commander, and on the evidence of the letters, the blame for this act has been assigned to him.

This stain on his reputation notwithstanding, he was made a knight of the Bath. After the death of his elder brother, Sackville, in 1763, he built a new country house, which he named Montreal, on the family estate near Sevenoaks. But in 1768 a growing colonial discontent led King George III to the conclusion that Amherst should be governor in Virginia. Amherst did not accept. Seven years later, with worse trouble brewing in the American colonies, the king pressed him to take the command in North America. For reasons that remain uncertain, he declined. In 1778, with the American Revolution two years old, the king named him Baron Amherst of Holmesdale, thereby making him Lord Amherst. As the urging of his ministers in 1778, the king again asked him to take command in America, and again he refused. Later that year, he was appointed in effect the commander in chief of the British army, and in June 1780 he had the task of restoring order when London was ravaged by riots. At the beginning of 1793 as another war with France was approaching, the seventy-six-year-old Amherst was officially appointed commander in chief with a seat in the cabinet. He retired again two years later. He was promoted to field marshal on July 30, 1796, and he died on August 3, 1797.

As he was being buried in the parish church of Sevenoaks, Americans who had learned about Freemasonry and how to fight a guerrilla-type war while serving in his army were engaged in the writing of a constitution for the United States of America, whose birth they'd proclaimed in 1776 in a Declaration of Independence signed by several men who counted themselves in the "brotherhood" of Freemasonry.

When nonmilitary Masonic lodges were established in New Jersey, New York, and Pennsylvania, they were "irregular," meaning that they had not been chartered by the Grand Lodge of England. The first to be given a grant of "warrant" from England's Grand Master (Lord Montague) was in Boston, Massachusetts. It was presented to Henry Price on July 30, 1733. At a meeting on that day in the Bunch of Grapes Tavern, he and several now formally recognized "brethren" claimed the title "first Lodge in Boston" and named it "St. John's Grand Lodge." None of the members of the Boston lodge had ever been employed in stone working. They were attracted to Freemasonry by its intellectual, philosophical, and religious aspects and by the opportunities membership afforded for convivial social intercourse. These sentiments of Masonic fraternity among members of St. John's Lodge would be tested in 1752 in the form of a rival lodge that was sanctioned by the Grand Lodge of Scotland.

Macoy notes that "the prayer of the petitioners being granted, they received a dispensation, dated Nov. 30, 1752, from Sholto Charles Douglas, Lord Aberdour, then Grand Master. It constituted them a regular Lodge under the title of 'St. Andrew's Lodge, No. 82,' to be holden in the province of Massachusetts Bay." Installed as grand master of the new lodge was Dr. Joseph Warren. Among the members were Boston silversmith Paul Revere, attorney-at-law John Hancock, and other figures who would be recorded and venerated in the history of the United States and called the Founding Fathers.

Chapter 2

The Knights Templar of America

T O SOME MUSLIMS AND ISLAMIC FUNDAMENTALIST FOLLOWERS, terrorists, members of Al Qaeda, and other "jihadist" groups at the start of the twenty-first century, it's as if the period of Crusaders battling for control of the Holy Land in the Middle Ages happened yesterday.

Since the destruction of King Solomon's Temple by the Babylonians in 486 B.C., the city of Jerusalem had been conquered and ruled by the Persians, Greeks, Romans, and the Christian Byzantine Empire until A.D. 638. In that year, a new power swept through the gates of the Holy City to take it over in the name of a new religion that had already claimed Arabia for its God, Allah. Led by Caliph Omar, the forces of Islam had defeated troops of the emperor Heraclitus in the Battle of Yarmuk on August 20, 636, and marched on to lay siege to the city until it surrendered in February 638. Because Mohammed, the founding prophet of Islam, had been miraculously taken into heaven from the city and returned to earth to promulgate the faith, the city was regarded as holy by Muslims. To venerate the prophet's journey, they built two sacred structures, the Dome of the Rock and the Al-Aqsa Mosque, on the ruins of Solomon's Temple and its successor that had been restored by King Herod and destroyed by the Romans in A.D. 70.

During two centuries of Islamic rule, relations between Muslims and Christians were amiable. This mutual toleration between the two religions ended in 1000, when the Christians of Europe heard reports from Jerusalem that Christian pilgrims and holy places were suffering at the hands of Muslims. Disturbed by these accounts and concerned about a growing threat to the Byzantine Empire by the westward spread of Islam, Pope Urban II, in a speech at the Council of Clermont in the spring of 1096, called on European powers to set aside internal disputes and rivalries to unite in a holy war to liberate the Holy City from the "infidels." The reward for those who took up arms in the name of Christ would be absolution and remission of sins. He declared, "God wills it."

The day after this exhortation, the council granted the privileges and protections that he promised. Those who took up arms to liberate Jerusalem adopted a red cross as their emblem and garnered the name "Crusaders." Setting out for the Holy Land, 60,000 soldiers and hordes of noncombatant peasants and pilgrims, with wives and children, were followed in the fall of 1096 by five more armies. After a year of arduous marching, the Crusaders were at Jerusalem's gates. When they took the city and thronged to the Church of the Holy Sepulchre (the traditional site of the Crucifixion and Resurrection), one of the leaders, Raymond of Agiles, saw a scene that would be "famous in all future ages, for it turned our labors and sorrows into joy and exultation." It was to him and his Crusader comrades a day of "justification of all Christianity, the humiliation of paganism, the renewal of faith."

Between 1096 and 1250, there would be seven Crusades. As they continued and many thousands of Christians made their way to and from Jerusalem, the pilgrimages were frequently attacked by Muslims. To provide protection for them, an order of warrior monks was founded in 1118 in France by Hugues de Payens, a knight of Burgundy, and Godefroid de St. Omer, a knight of southern France. They took a vow of poverty and the name "Poor Knights of Christ and of the Temple of Solomon." Given sanction by the Church in 1128 at the Council of Troyes, and with the support of St. Bernard of Clairvaux, the Templars became renowned for their ferocity in battle. Welcomed to the Holy City after the First Crusade by Baldwin I, the self-proclaimed king of Jerusalem, they were provided living space at the site of Solomon's Temple, hence the name "Templars."

Waging war on Muslims provided loot that not only left the Templars the richest men in Europe but also bankers to the king of France and the pope. This eventually resulted in the destruction of the order, execution of its leaders, and exile for survivors in Scotland. Over time, they called themselves Freemasons. The explanation for this transformation from warrior knights to Masons is attributed to a mingling of Templar precepts and Celtic mystery cults. The merger resulted in the Masonic Royal Order of Scotland. Known as the Scottish Rite, it would flourish in parts of Europe and eventually take root in America.

When a group of Boston Masons found themselves in disagreement in 1752 with what they called the "silk stocking" Masonry of the St. John's Grand Lodge that was approved by the Grand Lodge of England, they organized a more "democratic" group that was chartered by the Grand Lodge of Scotland (1756) and named it St. Andrew's Royal Arch Lodge. In a charter dated August 28, 1769, William Davis was recorded as "Accepted and Accordingly made by receiving the four steps" of Excellent, Super Excellent, Royal Arch, and Knight Templar.

Davis, who was thereby recognized as the first knight templar in America, was born in Boston on June 13, 1724. An Episcopalian, he owned an apothecary shop in Prince Street, was active in politics, and would play a significant role in the events leading up to the American Revolution. A member of the Committee on Correspondence in charge of "inspection and safety" in the Boston area, he was originally a member of the St. John's Lodge, then signed the petition to the Grand Lodge of Scotland that authorized St. Andrew's Lodge.

Outraged by the information of a rival body, St. John's membership "imagined their jurisdiction infringed" and refused any communications or visits from members of St. Andrew's. The rivalry was exacerbated in 1769 by the creation of the "Massachusetts Grand Lodge," with the assistance of three Masonic lodges within the ranks of the British army stationed in Boston. The new lodge conferred the degrees of Royal Arch and Knight Templar. At a "festival" held on May 30, 1769, a commission from the Earl of Dalhousie in his role of Grand Master of Masons in Scotland was given to Dr. Joseph Warren, appointing him Grand Master of Masons in Boston and within 100 miles of the city.

Describing these competing lodges in *The Temple and the Lodge,* the historians Michael Baigent and Richard Leigh observe, "Not surprisingly, things became acrimonious, tempers flared, a 'them against us' situation developed and a miniaturized civil war of Free-masonic insult ensued. St. John's looked askance at St. Andrew's and, with vindictive passion, repeatedly 'passed resolutions against it.' Whatever they entailed, these resolutions produced no effect and St. John's Lodge proceeded to sulk, petulantly forbidding its members to visit St. Andrew's."

America's second Knight Templar was Paul Revere, who was installed on December 11, 1769. (Warren was the third, on May 11, 1770.) Knight Templar degrees were also awarded in Pennsylvania, South Carolina, and Massachusetts. By May 13, 1805, there were enough knights to hold a convention in Providence, Rhode Island. They adopted a constitution and declared the "Grand Encampment of Knights Templar in the United States duly formed." After two centuries, the Knights Templar remain an important component of Freemasonry in the United States.

A modern brochure explains:

> The Knights Templar is a Christian-oriented fraternal organization that was founded in the 11th century. Originally, the Knights of Templar were laymen who protected and defended Christians traveling to Jerusalem. These men took vows of poverty, chastity and obedience, and were renowned for their fierceness and courage in battle. Today the Knights Templar display their courage and goodwill in other ways. They organize fund-raising activities such as breakfast, dinners, dances, and flea markets. They support Masonic-related youth groups and they raise millions of dollars for medical research and educational assistance.

Today's Templars are governed by the Grand Encampment of Knights Templar. State groups are called "Grand Commandery of Knights Templar." There are about 1,600 in the United States, Germany, Italy, and Mexico, with more than 260,000 members. Their motto is "Integrity, Obedience, Courage." In public ceremonies, the knights wear uniforms. Baigent and Leigh note that having conferred for the first time anywhere

in the world the degree of Knight Templar, St. Andrew's Lodge "continued to meet and to gain new recruits—sometimes, indeed, pilfering them
from St. John's."

Three years before the establishment of St. John's, the flourishing of
Freemasonry in the colonies was noted in a Philadelphia newspaper. On
December 8, 1730, the *Pennsylvania Gazette* referred to "several
Lodges of FREE MASONS erected in this Province." The owner, editor,
and printer of the *Gazette* was a former Bostonian. Born in 1706,
Benjamin Franklin was mostly self-taught and served an apprenticeship
to his father (a soap maker), then went to work for his half brother,
James. A printer, James founded the *New England Courant*, the fourth
newspaper in the colonies, to which Benjamin contributed fourteen es-
says. Because of some brotherly dissension, he left New England for
Philadelphia in 1723 and obtained employment as a printer. After a
year, he sailed to London and returned to Philadelphia two years later.
He rose rapidly in the printing trade and took over the *Pennsylvania
Gazette* from its founder. His most successful literary venture was
Richard's Almanac. By 1748, he was financially independent and recog-
nized for his philanthropy. When his Masonry articles appeared in the
Pennsylvania Gazette in 1730, he used the power of the press to ad-
vance a desire to join the fraternity. He became a member of St. John's
Lodge.

On November 28, 1734, Franklin wrote to the Boston lodge in reply
to a letter from Henry Price, its Grand Master. After noting that Price
had "so happily recovered" from an illness and wishing well to him and
"the prosperity of your whole Lodge," he turned to the legal status of
the lodge in Philadelphia. Stating that he had read "in Boston prints an
article of news from London" that Price's "power was extended over all
America," he appealed to Price to "give the proceedings and determina-
tions of our Lodge their due weight." Six months after it received a
charter, he was named Junior Warden of the Pennsylvania Grand Lodge,
and two years after that he was made Grand Master.

Franklin's lodge's meetings were held in Tun's Tavern. The meeting
place would gain another historical distinction in 1775 when the
Continental Congress authorized raising two battalions of a "United

States Marine Corps." The first volunteers were enlisted there. The leader of the group was Samuel Nicholas. A Freemason, he was born in Philadelphia in 1744 and became a successful businessman. Congress commissioned him "to organize and train five companies of marine forces, skilled in the use of small and large firearms, to protect America's ships at sea." They demonstrated their skills with forays in the Bahamas that captured military supplies. In the winter of 1776–1777, they aided General George Washington's small force in stealthily crossing the Delaware River from Pennsylvania in a surprise Christmas Eve 1777 attack on Hessian mercenaries at Trenton and later fought in the Battle of Princeton.

In 1743, Franklin held "fraternal communion" with his brethren in the First (St. John's) Lodge of Boston. Six years later, he was named Provincial Grand Master, an appointment that lasted one year. In 1755, he was present for the Quarterly Communication of the Grand Lodge of Massachusetts and prominent in the anniversary and dedication of the Freemason's Lodge in Philadelphia, the first Masonic building in America. Two years later, he went to London in the interest of Pennsylvania. Staying five years, he befriended leading intellectuals in England and Scotland, including the political and economic theorist Adam Smith, and contacted many English Freemasons. After returning to Philadelphia for two years, he was back in Britain in 1764. As a negotiator on behalf of the thirteen colonies concerning increasing tensions between them and King George III's government on the issue of taxation, he remained in London ten years. On January 29, 1774, he was summoned before the king's privy council, denounced as a thief and man without honor, and called to answer for an event that had occurred in Boston Harbor six weeks earlier.

On the night of December 16, 1773, a small group of men disguised as Mohawk Indians boarded the British East India Company's merchant ship *Dartmouth* to protest a tax on tea by dumping its cargo of 342 tea chests, valued at 10,000 pounds, into the harbor. Enshrined in U.S. history as the "Boston Tea Party," this milestone on the road to the Revolution is proudly claimed by Freemasonry as the work of members of St. Andrew's Lodge. The morning after the raid, St. Andrew's Lodge member and

Knight Templar Paul Revere mounted his horse to carry the news to New York. On the night of April 18, 1775, he would be in the saddle again to sound the alarm to "every Middlesex village and farm" that British troops were marching from Boston to seize caches of weapons at Concord. When the smoke of Battles at Lexington and Concord cleared and British soldiers were back in Boston, the stage was set for Freemasonry to claim its first American hero in the person of St. Andrew's Grand Master.

Chapter 3

Fraternity of Arms

BORN IN ROXBURY, MASSACHUSETTS, IN 1740, JOSEPH WAREN BE-
came a Mason in St. Andrew's Lodge on September 10, 1761. He
received the second degree on September 2, 1761. On November
28, 1765, he became a Master Mason. Described as "somewhat impetu-
ous in his nature, but brave to a fault," he spoke to a sizeable crowd at
Boston's Old South Church on the anniversary of the Boston Massacre
(March 3, 1770) with the knowledge that English army officers ususally
attended such gatherings to heckle the speaker. Describing that day, a
masonic biographer of Warren writes:

> It required a cool head and steady nerves, and Grand Master Joseph
> Warren had both. The crowd at the church was immense; the aisles,
> the pulpit stairs, and the pulpit itself was filled with officers and sol-
> diers of the garrison, always there to imitidate the speaker. Warren
> was equal to the task but entered the church through a pulpit win-
> dow in the rear, knowing he might have been barred from entering
> through the front. In the midst of his most impassioned speech, an
> English officer seated on the pulpit stairs and in full view of Warren,
> held several pistol bullets in his open hand. The act was significant;
> while the moment was one of peril and required the exercise of both
> courage and prudence, to falter and allow a single nerve or muscle
> to tremble would have meant failure—even ruin to Warren and oth-
> ers. Everyone present knew the intent of the officer but Warren hav-
> ing caught the act of the officer and without the least discomposure

or pause in his discourse, simply approached the officer and dropped a white handkerchief into the offier's hand! The act was so cleverly and courteously performed that the officer was compelled to acknowledge it by letting the orator to continue in peace.

Elected major general by the Provincial Congress of Massachusetts on June 14, 1775, with no military education or experience, Warren was placed in command of the rebel force on Breed's Hill (later called Bunker Hill) as the "Red Coats" crossed the bay from Boston to lift a siege of the city that had been established after Lexington and Concord. Despite protests by Generals Artemis Ward and Israel Putnam, Warren shouldered a musket behind barricades on the hill.

The shooting on June 17, 1775, lasted less than an hour, with the Americans running out of ammunition. Warren was shot in the back of the head and killed. His body was thrown in a ditch by a British officer and buried with several other bodies. Discovered months later, Warren's body was identified by Paul Revere by a false tooth that he had made for American Freemasonry's first knight templar "martyr" in the cause of independence.

It was at Bunker Hill that William Davis, the original American templar, invented what was known as "the barrel defense." It consisted of barrels packed with stones and earth that were rolled down the hill at the British attackers. The richest Bostonian of his day while still in his twenties, with interests in shipping and real estate, Davis was enrolled in an "independent company" of Bostonians in a regiment under Major General John Hancock. He was born in 1737. After his father's death, he was adopted by an uncle, a wealthy Boston merchant whose business he entered after graduating from Harvard in 1754. Admitted to Merchants Lodge No. 277 in Quebec on January 26, 1762, he affiliated with Boston's St. Andrew's Lodge on October 14, 1762. He was a leader in the struggle against British taxation. In 1768, he refused to allow royal inspectors aboard his ship, the *Liberty*. This brought about the seizure of the vessel, followed by a riot in Boston. Defiance of the British won him great popularity, and in 1769 he was elected to the Massachusetts General Court. Six years later he was chosen to be a delegate to the second

Continental Congress and served as its president from 1775 to 1776. It was in this role that he became the first signer of the Declaration of Independence. He wrote his name large and with a flourish, explaining that he did this so King George III would be able to read it without putting on his spectacles.

Another wealthy Massachusetts businessman and Freemason who enthusiastically joined the fight for independence was John Glover. Born in 1732 in Marblehead, Massachusetts, he made his fortune in fishing and merchandising and was commissioned to lead the Marblehead regiment after the Battle of Lexington. His men were trained for naval operations and took part in an evacuation by boat of Washington's force from Long Island to Manhattan. They later ferried Washington and his troops across the Delaware for the Christmas Eve surprise attack on Trenton, then carried 750 captured Hessians to Pennsylvania.

New Hampshire–born Freemason John Stark had served as a lieutenant under Jeffrey Amherst in the French and Indian War. A colonel at Bunker Hill, he later helped fortify New York after the retreat from Long Island, participated in an expedition to Canada, and took part in the Battles of Morristown and Short Hills, New Jersey. When he died in 1822, he was the last surviving general of the Revolution.

William Whipple was born in Maine but became a New Hampshire merchant. Serving as a brigadier general in the New Hampshire militia, he took the surrender of British general John Burgoyne at the Battle of Saratoga. Another businessman, Mordecai Gist of Maryland, organized the Baltimore Independent Company Militia and was engaged in several battles. He attended a convention of military lodges in Morristown, New Jersey, in 1780, at which a resolution to create an American grand lodge with George Washington as the Supreme Grand Master failed to pass. It was the closest American Freemasonry came to establishing a national Grand Lodge.

General Hugh Mercer was born in Scotland, received a medical education, and joined the British army as a surgeon's mate. Immigrating to America, he set up a practice in Pensylvania and learned about Freemasonry and battle tactics while fighting in the French and Indian War. During the war, he met George Washington, who persuaded him to move to Fredericksburg, Virginia, where he was admitted to Masonic Lodge No. 4. A brigadier general, he was killed at the Battle of Princeton after his horse was shot out from under him.

Another Freemason, friend of George Washington, and son of the founder of the Lutheran Church in America, John Peter Gabriel Muhlenberg of Pennsylvania became a Lutheran pastor in New Jersey. He famously said in a sermon before he became a colonel, "There is a time for all things—a time to preach and a time to pray; but there is also a time to fight, and that time has now come."

While serving as a volunteer during the French and Indian War, Massachusetts-born Israel Putnam became a Mason in a military lodge. Captured by Indians, he was rescued by the French and released in a prisoner exchange. As a farmer in Connecticut, he learned of the Battles of Lexington and Concord while cultivating a field. He abandoned the plow, mounted his horse, and rode to Massachusetts. Put in charge of training volunteers by Joseph Warren, he was at his side when the pioneering American Freemason and Knight Templar was killed. Putnam also has the distinction of being the only major general to serve in the war from start to finish.

The history of blacks in American Masonry began when Prince Hall was initiated into the Irish Constitution Military Lodge along with fifteen other free black men. Little is known of his early life. He was probably born in Barbados, West Indies, on September 12, 1748. He may have arrived in Boston from Africa in 1765 as a slave and was sold to William Hall, who freed him in 1770. During the war, he served in the Continental army and is believed to have fought at Bunker Hill. Initiated into Military Lodge No. 441 with fourteen others, he and the other initiates were granted authority to convene as African Lodge No. 1. Other members were Cyrus Johnson, Bueston Slinger, Prince Rees, John Canton, Peter Freeman, Benjamin Tiler, Duff Ruform, Thomas Santerson, Prince Rayden, Cato Speain, Boston Smith, Peter Best, Forten Howard, and Richard Titley.

At the end of the war, Hall petitioned the Premier Grand Lodge of England for a warrant. It was delivered to Boston on April 29, 1787. A week later (May 6, 1787), African Lodge No. 459 was organized. On

June 24, 1791, the African Grand Lodge of North America was organized in Boston with Prince Hall installed as Grand Master. A property owner and registered voter, he campaigned for the establishment of schools for Negro children in Boston, opened one in his own home, and successfully petitioned the state legislature to protect free Negroes from being kidnapped and sold into slavery. He died on December 4, 1807. The next year, as a memorial to him, and by an act of the General Assembly of the Craft, the lodge's name became Prince Hall Grand Lodge of Massachsetts.

Throughout the world today, there are 44 Most Worshipful Prince Hall Grand Lodges, about 5,000 subordinate lodges, and more than 300,000 Prince Hall Masons. For many years, the black churches of America and Prince Hall lodges were the strongest organizations in black communities. Masonic lodge halls were used as locations for church services and teaching blacks how to read and write. Prince Hall Masons used their resources to provide young men and women scholarships for college and to carry out various forms of charity in their local communities.

The American Revolution also saw the first American Indian initiated into Freemasonry. Named Thayendangea, he was the son of the chief of the Mohawks in the 1750s. He was brought up in the household of a prominent British administration official, Sir William Johnson, a Freemason, who gave him the name Joseph Brant. Having fought several battles with Johnson in the French and Indian War, he became Johnson's personal secretary. By the time of Johnson's death in 1774, he had become accepted by the British administration. When he went to England in 1775, he was made a Mason in a London lodge. Returning to America to enlist the Mohawks in the fight against the American rebels, he fought under the command of Colonel John Butler in several battles. But when prisoners who were turned over to the Mohawks to be tortured to death made Masonic signs, he released them. After the war, he became a member of St. John's Lodge of Friendship No. 2 in Canada, of which Butler had become Master, before returning to the Mohawks in Ohio.

Analyzing the influence of Freemasonry on the course of the War for Independence in *The Temple and the Lodge,* Baigent and Leigh find it both direct and oblique, general and in particular. "In a less direct, less quantifiable fashion," they write, "it helped to create a general atmosphere, a psychological climate or ambience which helped shape the thinking not only of active brethren such as Franklin and Hancock, but of non-Freemasons as well." Principles of liberty, equality, brotherhood, tolerance, and "the rights of man," reasoned Baigent and Leigh, "would not have had the currency they did" without the prevalence of Freemasonry throughout Britain's American colonies. It imparted its attitudes and values to the newly formed Continental army and may have had something to do with the appointment of Washington as commander in chief. Charles Wilson Peale, the era's most famous portrait painter and a Freemason, would render likenesses of Revolutionary War Freemasons, including Hancock and Franklin, but his best known of several portraits he did of George Washington is on the front of the dollar bill.

Chapter 4

Brother Washington

BORN IN VIRGINIA ON FEBRUARY 22, 1732, GEORGE WASHINGTON became a Freemason in the lodge at Fredericksburg, Virginia, on August 4, 1753, at age twenty-one. When a lodge was chartered in Alexandria in 1788, he was named Charter Master. As president of the United States, he wrote to a lodge in Rhode Island in 1790, "Being persuaded that a just application of the principles on which the Masonic Fraternity is founded must be a promotive of private virtue and public prosperity, I shall always be happy to advance the interest of the Society and to be considered by them as a deserving brother."

Although he wrote letters indicating that he was happy to be a Freemason and that he never sought to resign or repudiate his Masonic membership, there is little to no evidence that he attended many Masonic lodge meetings after his initiation in 1753 but he may have attended the dinners. He seems not to have participated in meetings of the lodge of which he was the first Master of what today is called Alexandria-Washington Lodge No. 22. While Master of the lodge, he did not assist in the work of the lodge. In one puzzling letter he denied that he was a Mason.

As commander in chief of the army, he was virtually surrounded by Masons. Half of his generals belonged to the Craft, including France's Marie-Paul de Lafayette and the Prussian army officer Baron Friedrick von Steuben.

While they battled with regular English troops and mercenaries on land, John Paul Jones, a young seagoing Freemason who was born in

Scotland and had embraced the American cause, carried the fight to the high seas by attacking British shipping and raiding English ports. Revered as the father of the U.S. Navy, Jones gave Americans one of their most stirring battle cries: "I have not yet begun to fight."

While Freemasons are justifiably proud of Masons who served gallantly in the War for Independence, one of its most brilliant and heroic generals proved to be an embarrassment. Early in the war, Benedict Arnold (initiated in Connecticut in 1763) distinguished himself by leading an asault on Quebec, Canada. Wounded in the leg in the bold attack that failed to take the city, he emerged as a hero. During the Battle of Saratoga, he proved to be a brilliant strategist who again exhibited heroics. But the commander, General Horatio Gates, a Mason, relieved him of his command, in part for insubordination and in part because Gates viewed Arnold as a "pompous little fellow." This insult to Arnold was assuaged following British abandonment of Philadelphia when Washington appointed him to the post of commandant of the city. But by this time he was an embittered figure with open disdain for his fellow officers and deep resentment toward Congress for not promoting him more quickly.

Arnold was also a widower who courted and married Margaret (Peggy) Shippen. Described as "a talented young woman of good family," at nineteen she was half Arnold's age and pro-British. Plunging into the social life of America's largest and most sophisticated city by throwing lavish parties, Arnold was soon deeply in debt. This drew him into dubious financial schemes that caused Congress to investigate his activities, resulting in a recommendation that he be brought before a court-martial. He complained to Washington that having "become a cripple in the service of my country, I little expected to meet ungrateful returns."

Confronted with personal and financial ruin, facing an uncertain future of promotion, and disgusted with politicians in Congress, Arnold made a fateful and ultimately ruinous decision to wipe out his troubles by offering his services to the British. Writing to their commander, Sir Henry Clinton, a Mason, he promised to deliver to the British the garrison at West Point, with 3,000 defenders, in the belief that the surrender would bring about the collapse of the American cause. To put himself in a position to do so, Arnold persuaded Washington to place the fort under his command. In September 1780, he was ready to act. To assist him in the plot the British chose Major John André, a Mason, as the go-between. The two men shared more than the conspiracy to neutralize West Point. Before Arnold married Shippen, André had been her suitor.

Serving with the Fifty-fourth Foot as adjutant general to General Clinton, André was also in charge of British spy operations. The plot involved coded letters and invisible ink. To make it easier for the British to take over, Arnold scattered his troops to weaken West Point's defenses. Following a meeting with Arnold on September 21, 1780, André set out for his own lines in civilian clothes and carrying identification papers in the name of "John Anderson." He was stopped by three suspicious Americans, taken to headquarters, searched, and exposed as a spy. Learning this, Arnold hastened to New York and the safety of his British allies.

When the British expressed a desire to gain André's release, Washington sent Aaron Ogden, a prominent political leader (and Mason), to inform General Clinton that he would release André only in exchange for Arnold. Clinton refused and André was hanged on October 2, 1780. He accommodated his executioner by placing the noose around his neck and tying his own handkerchief as a blindfold. His body was eventually disinterred and buried with much pomp as a hero in Westminster Abbey.

Chapter 5

Cornerstones of Government

RECALLING THE SIGNING OF THE DECLARATION OF INDEPENDENCE, Freemason William Ellery wrote, "I was determined to see how they all looked as they signed what might be their death warrant. I eyed each closely as he affixed his name to the document. Undaunted resolution was displayed in every countenance."

Sixteen of the fifty-six signers (28 percent) of the Declaration of Independence were either Masons or probable ones. The known are Benjamin Franklin, John Hancock, Joseph Hewes, William Hooper, Robert Treat Payne, Richard Stockton, George Walton, William Whipple, and Ellery. Those for whom there is evidence of Masonic membership or affiliations were Elbridge Gerry, Lyman Hall, Thomas Nelson Jr., John Penn, George Read, Roger Sherman, and Thomas Jefferson.

While the Declaration was being discussed in June 1776, Congress took time out to appoint a committee to prepare plans for treaties "of commerce and amity" with other countries. When it issued a report in September, Congress presented the task to three "commissioners." It named Silas Deane, who was already in Europe, Jefferson, and Franklin.

As an envoy to France, Franklin formed affiliations with the country's Masonic lodges. In 1777, he was elected a member of the Lodge des Neuf Souers (Lodge of the Nine Sisters, or Nine Muses) of Paris, and in 1778 he assisted in Voltaire's initiation into the lodge. In 1782, he became a member of Lodge de Saint Jean de Jerusalem. In the following year, he was elected venerable d'honneur of that body. The same year, he was made an honorary member of Lodge des bons Amis (Good Friends),

Rouen. These and other distinctions were honored in a sermon at St. Paul's Church, Philadelphia. On St. John's Day in December 1786, he was referred to as "an illustrious Brother whose distinguished merit among Masons entitles him to their highest veneration." One scholar of Franklin's contributions to Masonry writes that no catalog of his offices, services, dates, names, and places could adequately convey his importance and "facets of a many-sided jewel which best reflect the influence Freemasonry had upon him."

Franklin wrote, "Freemasonry has tenets peculiar to itself. They serve as testimonials of character and qualifications, which are only conferred after our course of instruction and examination. These are of no small value; they speak a universal language, and act as a passport to the attentions and support of the initiated in all parts of the world. They cannot be lost as long as memory retains its power." He also observed, "Masonic labor is purely a labor of love. He who seeks to draw Masonic wages in gold and silver will be disappointed. The wages of a Mason are earned and paid in their dealings with one another; sympathy that begets sympathy, kindness begets kindness, helpfulness begets helpfulness, and these are the wages of a Mason."

During the convention in Philadelphia that produced the U.S. Constitution, Franklin used language that Freemasons interpret as evidence of his Masonry:

> The longer I live, the more convincing proofs I see of this truth, that God governs in the affairs of men. And if a sparrow cannot fall to the ground without his notice, is it probable that an empire can rise without His aid? We have been assured, Sir, in the Sacred Writings, that "except the Lord build the house, they labor in vain that build it." I firmly believe this; and I also believe, that, without His concurring aid, we shall succeed in this political building no better than the builders of [the Tower of] Babel.

A Masonic Franklin biographer writes: "It is not for us to say what he would have been had there been no Freemasonry in his life; it is for us only to revere the Franklin who was among the very greatest of any other nation, in all times; for us to congratulate ourselves and be thankful for our country, that this wise philosopher, this leader of men and of nations, had taken to his heart the immutable and eternal principles of the Ancient Craft."

On November 15, 1777, representatives of the former colonies voted to adopt thirteen Articles of Confederation and sent them to the states for ratification. Because of Maryland's refusal to agree until states claiming western lands ceded them to the new nation, approval did not occur until March 1, 1781. With independence secured by the surrender of the British force under General Charles Cornwallis to General George Washington at Yorktown, Virginia, on August 19, 1782, Americans had won their independence, but as the Masonic historian H. C. Clausen notes in *Masons Who Helped Shaped Our Nation,* "Though free, we were not yet united. The loose Article of Confederation did not provide a strong national government, common currency or consistent judicial system. Men of vision realized that another step must be taken if the weak Confederation of American States was to become a strong, unified nation."

In the calling for a convention to devise a new structure of governance, and during the debate that resulted in the formation of the U.S. Constitution, Freemasons played a significant role. When a Constitutional Convention opened on May 25, 1787, in Philadelphia, with eighty-one-year-old Benjamin Franklin as a delegate and George Washington the unanimous choice of fifty-five representatives as presiding officer, Freemasonry was not only the single remaining pre-Revolution fraternal entity but also the sole organization operating nationally. More than two and a half centuries later, in the paper "Masonic Education and Service for the Grand Lodge of Texas," the Masonic scholar James Davis Carter observes, "The role of Freemasonry and individual Masons prior to and through the American Revolution was that of the destruction of the traditional social and political order based on an authoritarian philosophy and characterized by inequality and privilege."

With the victorious end of the American Revolution, Carter notes, "philosophy had, for the first time in history, an opportunity to play a constructive role in the erection of a political and social order. The experience of Masonic organizations before the Modern Age had taught

Masons that liberty for the individual has never been handed down by the government—that liberty is gained through the limitation of the powers of government, not the increase of them."

Carter continues:

> Masons had also discovered that freedoms are learned—the individual has freedom of thought only as he learns to move within the limits established by a rational intelligence; he has freedom to form opinions only after he has learned to distinguish the true from the false; he has social freedom only after he has learned to live according to accepted standards of social intercourse; he has political freedom to the extent to which the law protects his political rights; and he has freedom to extend his liberties only when he has learned to fulfill obligations and conditions of those liberties. Masons have long recognized that the "discovery of the power to aim at ideal ends freely chosen by his own will and intelligence is the supreme achievement of man, and in that, more than any other in any other single fact, lies hope of the future."

This traditional Masonic analysis of the Constitution continues:

> Included in [the first ten] amendments were principles advocated by Masons, including religious toleration, freedom of speech, a speedy trial according to law before equals when accused of law violation, no imposition of excessive punishment, reservation of all powers not delegated in the Constitution. A comparison of the principles of government universally adopted by Masons, with those contained in the Constitution, reveals they are essentially the same in both documents. There is conclusive evidence that the majority of the men who worked for a federal union and wrote the Constitution were Masons. Some of these Masons were the most influential leaders of the fraternity in America, fully conversant with Masonic principles of government. Freemasonry was the only institution at that time governed by a federal system. There is not a scrap of evidence left by any member of the Constitutional Convention indicating

that these principles were drawn from any other source. Since the government of the United States bears such a startling similarity to the government of the Masonic fraternity in theory and in structure, it is difficult to ascribe the similarity to coincidence.

On June 21, 1778, New Hampshire became the required ninth state to ratify the new Constitution. On July 2, the last Congress under the Articles of Confederation resolved that the states should choose presidential electors on the first Wednesday in January 1789, that one month later they should select a president and vice president, and that a congress elected under the Constitution should meet the first Wednesday in March in New York. The unanimous choice for president was Washington, with John Adams, a non-Mason, as vice president. On April 30, 1789, Washington's oath of office was administered by Chancellor Robert R. Livingston, Grand Master of the Grand Lodge of New York. General Jacob Morton, Worshipful Master of St. John's Lodge—the oldest in the city—and Grand Secretary of the Grand Lodge of New York, served as marshal of the inauguration ceremonies.

When Washington recited the presidential oath of office as required by the Constitution, the Bible was opened to Genesis, chapters 49 and 50, consisting of the prophecies of Jacob concerning his sons and his son Joseph's death. Printed by Mark Baskett, "Printer to the King's Most Excellent Majesty," in London in 1767, the Bible's first page bore a steel-engraved portrait of King George II. The second page was inscribed, "On this sacred volume, on the 30th day of April, A. L. 5789, in the City of New York, was administered to George Washington, the first president of the United States of America, the oath to support the Constitution of the United States. This important ceremony was performed by the Most Worshipful Grand Master of Free and Accepted Masons of the State of New York, the Honorable Robert R. Livingston, Chancellor of the State." This was followed with:

> *Fame stretched her wings and with her trumpet blew*
> *Great Washington is near. What praise is due?*
> *What title shall he have? She paused and said*
> *"Not one—his name alone strikes every title dead."*

A King James version, complete with the Apocrypha and elaborately supplemented with the historical, astronomical, and legal data of that period, the Bible contained numerous artistic steel engravings portraying biblical narratives from designs and paintings by old masters and engraved by the celebrated English artist John Stuart. It had been presented to the lodge by Jonathan Hampton on November 28, 1770.

This Bible was used at the inaugurations of Presidents Warren Harding (1921), Dwight D. Eisenhower (1953), Jimmy Carter (1977), and George H. W. Bush (1989). It was also to have been used for the inauguration of George W. Bush in 2001, but rain prevented it. It has also been present at numerous public and Masonic occasions. They include Washington's funeral procession in New York, December 31, 1799; dedication of the Masonic Temple in Boston, June 24, 1867, and in Philadelphia in 1869; the dedication of the Washington Monument, February 21, 1885 (and its rededication in 1998); and the laying of the cornerstone of the Masonic Home at Utica, May 21, 1891. It was also used at the opening of the present Masonic Hall in New York on September 18, 1909, when St. John's Lodge held the first meeting, and conferred the first Third Degree in the newly completed temple. It was displayed at the 1964 World's Fair in New York, at the Central Intelligence Agency headquarters in Langley, Virginia, and at the *Famous Fathers and Sons* exhibition at the George H. W. Bush Memorial Library in Texas in 2001. When not in use by St. John's Lodge or on tour, it is on permanent display in what is now Federal Hall in New York, where Washington took the oath.

Of those who accompanied Washington in the inauguration ceremony, Roger Sherman, Alexander Hamilton, Baron Friedrich von Steuben, General Henry Knox, and John Adams, all except Adams were Masons. The governors of the thirteen states at the time of Washington's inauguration were Masons. Washington chose for his first cabinet men who were Masons or sympathetic to the Craft's ideals: Thomas Jefferson became secretary of state; Alexander Hamilton, secretary of the treasury; General Henry Knox, secretary of war; and Edmund Randolph (the grand master of the Grand Lodge of Virginia in 1788), attorney general. While they were chosen because of their fitness for public office, in the minds of Washington and other men of that time Masonic membership was another evidence of a man's reliability and fitness for trust. Washington wrote that "being persuaded that a just application of the principles on which the Masonic fraternity is founded must be promotive of private virtue and public prosperity, I shall always be happy to advance the interests of the Society and be considered by them a deserving Brother." One of Washington's first duties was to appoint the chief justice and four associate justices of the Supreme Court. Four were Masons: Chief Justice John Jay and Associate Justices William Cushing, Robert H. Harrison, and John Blair.

The first Congress elected under the Constitution had several Masons. In the House of Representatives were Abraham Baldwin, Theodorick Bland, John Brown, Daniel Carroll, Elbridge Gerry, Frederick A. Muhlenberg, John Page, Josiah Parker, John Sevier, Nicholas Gilman, Thomas Hartly, James Jackson, John Lawrence, James Madison, Roger Sherman, William Smith, John Steele, Thomas Sumter, and Jeremiah van Rensselaer. Muhlenberg was elected Speaker of the House. Of twenty-six senators, thirteen are known to have been Freemasons: Oliver Ellsworth, James Gunn, William S. Johnson, Samuel Johnston, Rufus King, John Langdon, Richard Henry Lee, James Monroe, Robert Morris, William Paterson, George Read, and Phillip Schuyler

Freemasons find connections between Masonry and the U.S. government in the Declaration of Independence and Constitution. Pointing out that many leaders in the development of the federal union were Masons, they claim that the idea of a free public school system supported by the state was fostered by Masons. The policy of admitting new states to the Union on a basis of complete equality with the old, has a counterpart in Masonry in the creation of new lodges "equal in every respect to the position held by older lodges." Men who had an influence on the writing of the Constitution were Masons who were "well informed in Masonic philosophy, practice and organization." Freemasons occupied influential offices in the executive, legislative, and judicial branches of the government at the birth of the nation.

On September 25, 1793, Washington left New York for the laying of the cornerstone of the Capitol building in a city that had been named for him in the federal District of Columbia. He was, said the *Columbian*

Mirror and *Alexandria Gazette,* the central figure in "one of the grandest MASONIC Processions" ever seen. The newspaper reported:

> About 10 o'clock, Lodge, No. 9, were visited by that Congregation, so graceful to the Craft, Lodge, No. 22, of Virginia, with all their Officers and Regalia, an directly afterwards appeared on the southern banks of the Grand River Potomack: one of the finest companies of Volunteer Artillery that has been lately seen, parading to receive the President of the United States, who shortly came in sight with his suite—to whom the Artillery paid their military honors, and his Excellency and suite crossed the Potomack, and was received in Maryland, by the Officers and Brethren of No. 22, Virginia and No. 9, Maryland whom the President headed, and preceded by a bank of music; the rear brought up by the Alexandria Volunteer Artillery; with grand solemnity of march, proceeded to the President's square in the City of Washington: where they were met and saluted, by No. 15, of the City of Washington, in all their elegant regalia, headed by Brother Joseph Clark, Rt. W.G.M.— P.T. and conducted to a large Lodge, prepared for the purpose of their reception. After a short space of time, by the vigilance of Brother C. Worthy Stephenson, Grand Marshall, P.T. the Brotherhood and other Bodies were disposed in a second order of procession, which took place amid a brilliant crowd of spectators of both sexes.

The assemblage consisted of the surveying department of the city of Washington; the mayor and officials of "George-Town"; the Virginia Artillery; the commissioners of the city of Washington and their attendants; stone cutters; mechanics; two sword bearers; Masons of the first, second, and third degree; bearers of "Bibles &c on the Grand Cushions"; stewards with wands; a band; Lodge No. 22 of Virginia, "disposed in their own order"; bearers of corn, wine, and oil; "Grand Master P. T. [Prince of the Tabernacle] George Washington, W.M. [Worshipful Master] No. 22, Virginia"; and a "Grand Sword Bearer."

The newspaper account continued:

The procession marched two a-breast, in the greatest solemn dignity, with music playing, drums beating, colors flying, and spectators rejoicing; from the President's Square to the Capitol, in the City of Washington; where the Grand Marshall called a halt, and directed each file in the procession, to incline two steps, one to the right, and one to the left, and face each other, which formed a hollow oblong square; through which the Grand Sword Bearer led the van; followed by the Grand Master P.T. on the left—the President of the United States in the Centre, and the Worshipful Master of Number 22, Virginia, on the right—all the other orders, that composed the procession advanced, in the reverse of their order of march from the President's Square, to the south-east corner of the Capitol; and the Artillery filed off to a defined ground to display their maneuvers and discharge their cannon: The President of the United States, the Grand Master, P.T. and the Worshipful M. of No. 22, taking their stand to the East of a huge stone; and all the Craft, forming a circle westward, stood a short time in silent lawful order. The Artillery discharged a Volley. The Grand Marshall delivered to the Commissioners, a large Silver Plate with an inscription thereon which the commissioners ordered to be read, and was as follows:

> This South East corner stone, the Capitol of the United States of America in the City of Washington, was laid on the 18th day of September 1793, in the thirteenth year of American Independence, in the first year of the second term of the Presidency of George Washington, whose virtues in the civil administration of his country have been as conspicuous and beneficial, as his Military valor and prudence have been useful in establishing her liberties, and in the year of Masonry 5793, by the Grand Lodge of Maryland, several Lodges under its jurisdiction, and Lodge No. 22, from Alexandria, Virginia. Thomas Johnson, David Stuart and Daniel Carroll, Commissioners, Joseph Clark, R.W.G.M. pro tem., James Hobam and Stephen Hallate, Architects. Collin Williamson, Master Mason.

The Artillery discharged a volley. The Plate was then delivered to the President, who, attended by the Grand Master pro tem., and three Most worshipful Masters, descended to the cavazion trench and deposited the plate, and laid it on the corner-stone of the Capitol of the United States of America, on which were deposited corn, wine, and oil, when the whole congregation joined in reverential prayer, which was succeeded by Masonic chanting honors, and a volley from the Artillery.

The whole company retired to an extensive booth, where an ox of five-hundred pounds weight was barbecued, of which the company generally partook with every abundance of other recreation. The festival concluded with fifteen successive volleys from the Artillery.... Before dark the whole company departed with joyful hopes of the production of their labor.

The laying of the Capitol cornerstone occurred on a date between publication of the first edition of *Ilustrosions of Masonry* by William Preston in 1772 in London and the first edition of *The Freemason's Monitor* (a version of Preston adopted for American Freemasonry) by Thomas Smith Webb in 1797 in Albany, New York. Preston's publication was available to the Masons who planned the Capitol cornerstone laying. More familiar to the planners would have been John K. Read's *New Ahiman Rezon,* published in Richmond, Virginia, in 1791, two years before the Capitol event. It was published for the guidance of the Virginia lodges and dedicated to "George Washington, Esq. President of the United States of America."

Visual proof of Washington's Freemasonic observation was provided in a portrait by William Williams in 1794. At the request of the Alexandria Lodge, Washington stood for the painting wearing Masonic regalia. Documents show that on March 18, 1797, he "received" a delegation from the Alexandria Lodge, and on April 1, 1798, he attended a lodge banquet and proposed a toast.

Although his last will and testament expressed his desire "that my Corpse may be Interred in a private manner, without parade, or funeral Oration," his lodge was permitted to prepare arrangements for the funeral procession. Mourners were instructed to arrive at Mount Vernon on Wednesday "at twelve o'clock, if fair, or on Thursday at the same hour." Early on Wednesday, December 18, the Alexandria Lodge started for Mount Vernon and arrived about one o'clock. Two hours later the formal procession was formed, consisting of horse and foot soldiers, clergy, Washington's horse with an empty saddle, a military band, the bier, and dozens of mourners.

At a red brick tomb in a hillside below the mansion, the Reverend Thomas Davis, the rector of Christ Church, Alexandria, read the Episcopal Order of Burial. Next, the Reverend James Muir, the minister of the Alexandria Presbyterian Church, and Dr. Elisha Dick, both members of Washington's lodge, conducted the traditional Masonic funeral rites. The shroud was briefly withdrawn to allow a final viewing. A few days later, Muir wrote:

> In the long and lofty portico, where oft the hero walked in all his glory, now lay the shrouded corpse. The countenance, still composed and serene, seemed to depress the dignity of the spirit which lately dwelt in that lifeless form. There those who paid the last sad honors to the benefactor of his country took an impressive, a farewell view. Three general discharges of infantry, the cavalry, and eleven pieces of artillery, which lined the banks of the Potomac, back of the vault, paid the last tribute to the entombed Commander-in-Chief of the Armies of the United States.

Nearly half a century later, a ceremony in Pennsylvania was vividly recalled by Captain Samuel De Wees:

> Immediately after the arrival of [the] sad news [of his death], a public meeting was held at the court-House in [the town of] Reading, and arrangements made for a funeral procession. The Free Masons met at their Lodge, and made arrangements to join in the procession. A bright and exemplary brother had gone from a mystic Lodge upon earth, to join in membership with the Grand Lodge of transplendent and unconceived of brilliancy, holiness and glory above, and now, that the last funeral tribute was about to be paid, they could not be idle. Two companies of volunteers, one com-

manded by Captain Keims, were ordered out. The procession formed in the following order: the military in front, then the coffin, then the order of Masons, then civil officers, and then the citizens. The procession was fully a mile in length. It moved to a large church in Reading where the military, Masons and many of the citizens entered. The military moved (proceeded by the music) and placed the coffin in an aisle in front of the pulpit.

Washington would not have a memorial in his namesake capital city until many years after his death. Built at intervals between 1848 and 1885 with funds from public subscriptions and federal appropriations, a monument to honor him was considered during the Continental Congress in 1783. During the next three decades, Congress took no action on many additional proposals. In 1833, the Washington National Monument Society was organized by influential citizens who wanted a "great National Monument to the memory of Washington at the seat of the Federal Government."

By 1847, $87,000, including interest, had been collected. A design by architect Robert Mills was selected and provided for a decorated obelisk 600 feet high that was to rise from a circular colonnaded building 100 feet high and 250 feet in diameter. But this plan was altered during construction, so that the present monument has little in common with the Mills design. On July 4, 1848, the cornerstone was laid during a Masonic ceremony using the trowel Washington had wielded at the laying of the cornerstone of the Capitol in 1793.

In 1854, many people were dissatisfied with the work and collection of funds declined, largely because of growing antagonism between the North and South. This brought construction to a stop for almost a quarter of a century. The monument was left incomplete at the height of about 150 feet. It wasn't until August 2, 1876, that President Ulysses S. Grant approved an act committing the federal government to completion of the monument, with the Corps of Engineers of the War Department in charge of the work. When it resumed in 1880, Maryland marble facing was secured from the same vein as the original stone used for the lower portion. On August 4, 1884, the walls reached 500 feet. The capstone was set in place on December 6 and the monument was dedicated on February 21, 1885. It opened to the public on October 9, 1888. Inserted into the interior walls are 188 carved stones presented by individuals, societies, cities, states, and nations of the world.

Since its construction, critics of Freemasonry have discerned sinister, and even Satanic, symbolism. Noting that the number 3 has Masonic significance, they point out that the monument was built of 36,000 separate blocks of granite and that the number 36 is derived by multiplying 3 by 12. The capstone weighs exactly 3,300 pounds. As to the 188 specially donated memorial stones, those with suspicions of Freemasonry record that Masonic lodges throughout the world gave thirty-five that were mingled with the others, but that the last several were placed at the 330-foot level. These critics of Freemasonry claim that the cost of the monument, reported to be 1.3 million, is yet another instance of the Masonic number 13. The monument has eight windows that total thirty-nine square feet in size, a figure reached by multiplying 3 by 13. The figure 39 divided by 2 is 19.5, which is supposedly another significant Masonic number. The number 8 is purported to convey in occult numerology "new beginnings" and 13 means "extreme rebellion." This is seen as a "new beginning," that among Masons it is a euphemism for a "New World Order" through an "extreme rebellion," such as the Mason-inspired American Revolution. There are said to be other, more complicated Masonic numbers concealed within the construction of the monument that was constructed to honor the first Masonic president and designed so that both the White House and the Capitol face it. The obelisk was located at that place so that residents and visitors to the Capitol could face the obelisk daily. The monument is also described as part of a sinister Masonic design for the capital city itself that will be examined in a later chapter of this book.

During the period when the Washington Monument was slowly rising in fits and starts, the American style of Freemasonry was spreading as steadily as the continental country and the nation.

Chapter 6

Little Lodge on the Prairie

B Y THE TIME OF WASHINGTON'S DEATH, LODGES IN THE THIRTEEN states had become adherents of the Scottish Rite. Its earliest recording in America, at Washington's lodge in Fredericksburg, is dated December 22, 1753. Two years after his funeral, the Mother Supreme Council of the World was formed in Charleston, South Carolina (May 31, 1801). It established a thirty-third degree in the Scottish Rite, described by the Masonic historian C. W. Leadbeater in *Freemasonry and Its Ancient Mysteries* as "the most important and splendid of All Masonic Obediences."

After the Revolutionary War, a wave of Americans in search of land and bright opportunities began to move west. Masons took a prominent part in the exploration and settling of the new lands. On September 24, 1805, the Western Star Lodge No. 107 became the first lodge in the Indiana Territory. It held its first meeting in a two-story brick building that would later be rented to the state of Illinois to serve as the first state capitol.

By 1816, several Masonic lodges were operating in the Indiana Territory. They had been granted charters by the Grand Lodges of Pennsylvania, Kentucky, Tennessee, Missouri, and Indiana. A Masonic Convention on December 9, 1822, was held in the state capitol building at Vandalia. Several lodges in the territory that had been granted charters by the grand lodges of other states decided that since the territory had become a state in 1818, they should form their own grand lodge. Two days later, they proceeded to organize and nominate officers. They were presented to the lodges, approved, and duly elected. A year later, the Grand Lodge of Illinois met in "communication." From 1805 to 1827, eighteen lodges were formed in Illinois. One of the members recalled:

> Brothers that came two to four hours early started the fire to warm up the Lodge Room. This took cutting, splitting, hauling and stacking a lot of wood. Some of our Lodges hold on to the tradition of meeting as close to the full moon as possible. The quaint practice had the practical purpose of giving the Brothers coming home over those rutted and sometimes washed out roads a chance for their horse to see the hazards while they got some much needed sleep, having been up since before dawn to start the chores.

The gold rush fever of the Pikes Peak region of Colorado in 1858 attracted men of all descriptions—fortune-hunters, prospectors, and rovers—who were eager for quick wealth and excitement. A Masonic historian described a flood of

> hurriedly-formed wagon trains departing from Missouri river outposts thrown together for 700-mile, month-long journeys, men of every ilk, many of them fleeing from the rigidity of law and order and civilization. But its lure was irresistible to Masons, too. Many members of the craft responded to the sudden challenge of the frontier. And having been forced to associate with adventurers of dubious backgrounds during the tedious overland journey, upon arrival in the new country they quickly sought the company of their brethren.

Within ten days after the founding of the first permanent settlement at the junction of Cherry Creek and the Platte, the first informal assemblage of seven Masons was held in what was to be the territory and then the state of Colorado. Andrew Sagendorf, a member of that pioneering group, told the grand lodge in 1912 that the first meeting of Masonry in Denver was held in W. G. Russell's cabin on Perry street, near the site of the first bridge, early in November 1858. James Winchester presided, but because he was absent much of the time, Henry Allen generally occupied the Worshipful Master's station. No stated time or place of meeting was observed, so it was generally once a week and at the most secure and convenient cabin.

J. D. Ramage recalled:

> After being accosted by the salutation "Ho, that tent over there," from a man [Henry Allen], I accompanied Brother Allen to his abode, and there found brothers W. M. Slaughter, Dr. Russell, Andrew Sagendorf, and Oscar Lehow. These brethren together with Brother Allen and myself, made the first seven Masons, according to my knowledge and belief, who ever met in Colorado, having in contemplation the application for a charter, and a seven who stuck together, as Masons should do, through thick and thin.

They agreed to meet every Saturday night and "as our object in locating in Colorado was to get gold (we were supposed to be out prospecting during the week) we decided that any ideas concerning the country we were in which might come to us, news of mines we might discover, or any information which might be beneficial to the brethren, Masonically or financially, would at the next meeting, be given to the Masons there assembled."

In the deep South, a band of English colonists under the leadership of General James Edward Oglethorpe had arrived on the west bank of the Savannah River on February 12, 1733. This was the birth of the English province of Georgia, the last of the thirteen colonies, and the southwestern frontier of British America. On December 13, 1733, the Grand Lodge of England at its Quarterly Communication in London adopted a resolution to "collect the Charity of this Society towards enabling the Trustees [of Georgia] to send distressed Brethren to Georgia where they may be comfortably provided for." On February 21, 1734, a lodge was opened in Savannah, but without warrant. Noble Jones, a friend of Oglethorpe's, was initiated as the first Freemason in Georgia. On

December 2, 1735, the lodge was warranted by the Grand Lodge of England and entered on the engraved list as the "Lodge at Savannah in Ye Province of Georgia."

By 1892, there were fifty grand lodges in the United States, including one in the Indian Territory, which later became the Grand Lodge of Oklahoma It has been said that in every pioneer settlement of the West first came the church, then a school, then a Masonic lodge.

The Masonic scholar Duncan C. Howard, Past Grand Master in Texas, writes, "Masonry is the stuff from which good dreams come." Asserting that it dreams of a fatherhood of God, brotherhood of men, law and order and good citizenship in state, community, and nation, he continues, "No one seriously believes that Masonry has a monopoly on good citizenship. But the Masonic dream became the American dream as the early Masons in this nation faced the problems of a wild frontier." With motivation for law and order and motivation for better living in their community, pioneering Masons "became the motivators to establish free schools, free churches and Freemasonry wherever they lived."

This expansion of Freemasonry across the continent was stimulated by the Louisiana Purchase, negotiated on President Jefferson's behalf by Masons James Monroe, as secretary of state, and Robert R. Livingston, the New York Grand Master, who'd been on the committee with Jefferson, Benjamin Franklin, John Adams, and Roger Sherman that drafted the Declaration of Independence. He'd also administered Washington's oath of office.

Eager to learn everything he could about the region, Jefferson enlisted Meriwether Louis, a boyhood friend and personal secretary, and William Clark, a veteran of the Revolutionary War, to hastily organize "a corps of discovery" to lead the "Northwest Expedition."

Born in Charlottesville, Virginia, in 1774, Lewis served as a captain in several campaigns against the Indians. He attained Freemasonry's grand master degree in 1797 in Albemarle County's Virtue Lodge No. 44. When it went out of existence in 1801, he transferred to the Widow's Sons Lodge in Charlottesville. Clark was born in Caroline County, Virginia, in 1770. At age twenty-two, he joined the army of General

"Mad" Anthony Wayne as a lieutenant. He met Lewis during the 1794 campaign against the Indians and became a Mason with the formation of the St. Louis Lodge by men of the expedition.

With the dimensions and vast riches of this western territory revealed, Americans felt that they had a "manifest destiny" to first subdue it and then absorb it into the United States. Journeying from New York City to the Dakota Territory and becoming a rancher in 1886, an enthusiastic Freemason named Theodore Roosevelt gave voice to this objective. In a letter on June 7, 1897, to his friend John Hay, then America's ambassador to Great Britain, he wrote, "The young giant of the West stands in a continent and clasps the crest of an ocean in either hand. Our nation, glorious in youth and strength, looks into the future with eager eyes and rejoices as a string man to run a race." Initiated on January 2, 1901, by the Matinecock Lodge No. 806 in Oyster Bay, New York, he visited the Grand Lodge of Pennsylvania as president of the United States on November 5, 1902, for a celebration of the sesquicentennial of George Washington's Masonic initiation. Of his Masonic membership Roosevelt would say, "I enjoy going to some little lodge where I meet the plain hardworking people on the basis of genuine equality. It is the equality of moral men."

Freemasonry had reached Roosevelt's beloved Dakotas in 1862 at Yankton, the territorial capital, in the form of St. John's Lodge. Seven months later (July 31, 1863) it conducted the territory's first Masonic funeral. The deceased was Lieutenant Fredrick John Holt Beaver. Born in England and educated at Oxford, he was an Episcopal minister and volunteer soldier attached to the staff of General Henry H. Sibley. He was killed during a skirmish with Sioux Indians.

While the western frontier was being settled, Freemasons with a lust for adventure were heading north. In 1850, Elisha Kent Kane was a surgeon on the ship *Advance* that had embarked with another ship on a mission to locate an English exploration party that had disappeared during an attempt to reach the North Pole. In 1853, he was in command of *Advance* when it was trapped in ice. Kane led its crew to safety in

Greenland on foot. This feat was honored in Freemasonry in the United States with a lodge for explorers that bears his name.

Also venturing into the frozen north three decades later was one of the most famous and controversial explorers of the nineteenth century: General Adolphus W. Greeley. Born in Massachusetts in 1844, he was a Civil War veteran who between 1876 and 1879 was in charge of stringing more than 2,000 miles of telegraph line in Texas, the Dakotas, and Montana. Placed in command of building a chain of thirteen weather stations in Alaska in 1881, he would be regarded as a pioneer of the U.S. Weather service. When his construction team returned after becoming stranded and thought to be lost after three years, with all but seven having perished, the nation was shocked by a report that the others had been forced into cannibalism to survive. Greeley was also the father of the U.S. Army Signal Corps, and in 1906 he supervised army rescue and relief operations during and after the great earthquake that destroyed most of San Francisco. A member of St. Mark's Lodge, Newburyport, Massachusetts, and honorary member of Kane Lodge No. 454, called the Explorers Lodge, he was awarded the Congressional Medal of Honor shortly before his death in 1935.

The most famous Freemason-explorer was Robert E. Peary. A member of the Explorers Lodge, he started his career in exploration in Greenland, followed by Arctic adventures in the 1890s that culminated in him becoming the first man to reach the North Pole in 1909. In the party was Matthew A. Henson. Being a member of the Prince Hall "Celestial Lodge No. 3 of New York," Henson was Peary's chief assistant for twenty years. D. D. MacMillan, another member of the North Pole expedition, recalled, "As a carpenter, [Henson] built the sledges. A mechanic, he made alcohol stoves. An expert dog driver, he taught us how to handle our dogs. Highly respected by the Eskimos, he was easily the most popular man on board ship. Strong physically, and above all experienced, he was of more value to our Commander than all the rest of us put together. He went to the Pole with Peary because he was better than the rest of us."

Richard E. Byrd, the polar explorer, naval officer, and pioneer aviator, was the first man to fly over the North Pole. His Antarctic explorations between 1928 and 1935 resulted in numerous discoveries, including five mountain ranges and islands. Initiated into Freemasonry in 1921 at Federal Lodge No. 1, Washington D.C., he dropped Masonic flags on the North and South Poles. In the Antarctic odyssey of 1933–1935, the majority of the team were Masons (sixty out of eighty-two).

Having completed the work of the Corps of Discovery, Lewis and Clark each served as governor of the territory they'd explored and appointed a secretary, sheriff, and four judges, all of whom were Freemasons. Members of the Craft who also explored the western frontier were Kit Carson and Zebulon Pike.

While Lewis and Clark were off on their expedition, Pike and twenty men left from St. Louis in 1805 at Jefferson's behest to explore the headwaters of the Mississippi. Pike is best known for the Colorado mountain peak named after him. He was promoted to captain in August 1806, major in May 1808, lieutenant-colonel in 1809, and to full colonel in July 1812. As a military agent in New Orleans (1809–1810), he was deputy quartermaster-general and saw service in the War of 1812 as adjutant and inspector-general in the campaign against York (Toronto), Canada. In an attack on April 27, 1813, he had immediate command of the troops and was killed by a chunk of rock that fell on him when the retreating British garrison set fire to the powder magazine. Although his Masonic membership is questioned by some, Pike is credited by others with a membership in Lodge No. 3 in Philadelphia. His brother, Albert, would be a revolutionary figure in American Freemasonry.

In the years after Jefferson launched Lewis and Clark and Zebulon Pike on their treks into the land west of the Mississippi, lodges were founded west of the Appalachian Mountains in Ohio (1806), Louisiana (1812), Tennessee (1813), Indiana and Mississippi (1818), Missouri (1821), Arkansas (1832), Illinois (1820), Texas (1837), Wisconsin (1843), Iowa and Michigan (1844), Kansas and California (1850), Oregon (1852), Minnesota (1853), Nebraska (1847), Washington (1858), Colorado (1861), Nevada (1865), Idaho (1867), Utah (1872), the Indian Territory and Wyoming (1874), South Dakota (1875), New Mexico (1877), Arizona

(1882), North Dakota (1889), and Oklahoma Territory (1892). Between the formation of lodges in Illinois in 1820 and the creation of lodges in the 1840s, Freemasons who had thrived in their expansive country and anticipated even more success and growth found themselves under severe attack and Freemasonry in the United States being nearly driven to extinction.

Chapter 7

Backlash

IN WHAT ONE HISTORIAN CALLS "THE MOST ROMANTIC STORY OF Freemasonry," the events that culminated in a crisis for Freemasonry began in 1824 with the arrival of William Morgan in the town of Batavia. A native of Culpepper County, Virginia, he had worked it various jobs in Canada and called himself "Captain" because he claimed to have served with distinction in the War of 1812. A historian of American Masonry writes, "Accounts of him differ widely, as they do of any notorious person. Few are so wicked as to be without friends; few are so good they have not their detractors. From the estimates of both enemies and friends, the years have brought an evaluation of Morgan which shows him as a shiftless rolling stone; uneducated but shrewd; careless of financial obligations: often arrested for debt; idle and improvident; frequently the beneficiary of Masonic charity."

Records indicate that Morgan received the Royal Arch degree in Western Star Chapter No. 33, Le Roy, New York, on May 31, 1825. Masonic legend supposes that he "lied his way into a Lodge in Rochester by imposing on a friend and employer, who was led to vouch for him." What is known is that he visited lodges, was willing to assist in their work, made Masonic speeches, and took part in degrees. When Batavia Freemasons asked to be made a Royal Arch Chapter, he was among those signing the petition. When suspicion of his "regularity" began to spread, he was omitted as a member. He retaliated by asserting that he had written a book that would reveal Masonic secrets and boasted that he had a contract with three men for its publication: David C. Miller, an entered apprentice of twenty years' standing who been stopped from advancement "for cause"; John Davids, Morgan's landlord; and Russell Dyer, about whom little is known. The agreement guaranteed Morgan a half-million dollars.

According to a chronicler of these events, "Morgan boasted in bars and on the street of his progress in writing this book. The more he bragged, the higher the feeling against him ran, and the greater the determination engendered that the exposé should never appear. Brethren were deeply angered. Fearful that were the 'secrets' of Freemasonry 'exposed,' the Order would die out, feelings ran high."

When Morgan was arrested for the theft of a shirt and tie, in September 1826, he was acquitted, but immediately rearrested and jailed for failure to pay a debt of $2.68. After someone paid the debt, he left jail in a coach with several men and was taken to the fort (Niagara) and held in an unused ammunition magazine.

Upon his disappearance from Batavia, a rumor spread that Masons kidnapped and murdered him to prevent publication of his exposé. Freemasons denied the charge.

A few weeks later, a body floated to the shore of the Niagara River, about forty miles from the fort, and Morgan's wife identified the body based on the clothing. The mystery deepened when doubts were voiced concerning known markings on Morgan's body that were not on the corpse. Three inquests were held. The third decided that it wasn't Morgan, but Timothy Munro.

Before long three prime suspects, all local Masons, were arrested. Because kidnapping was merely a misdemeanor, none was sentenced to more than two years and four months.

The fact that Morgan had vanished after being abducted by Freemasons, combined with publication of the book they had sought to suppress, triggered an explosion of anti-Mason sentiment across the United States. The "fame and infamy of the Morgan affair," as one historian puts it, "grew and spread like wildfire." Anti-Mason meetings were held. The Craft was denounced by press and pulpit. The *Anti-Masonic Review,* an anti-Masonic paper, was published in New York. Groups in Pennsylvania, already opposed to any oath-bound society (e.g., the Quakers, Lutherans,

Mennonites, Dunkards, Moravians, Schwenkfelders, and members of the German Reformed Church), were aroused to "a high pitch of feeling" against Morgan's "murderers" and "kidnappers."

In 1903, Robert Freke Gould wrote in *History of Freemasonry: Its Antiquities, Symbols, Constitutions, Customs, etc.*:

> This country has seen fierce and bitter political contests, but no other has approached the bitterness of this campaign against the Masons. No society, civil, military or religious, escaped its influence. No relation of family or friends was a barrier to it. The hatred of Masonry was carried everywhere, and there was no retreat so sacred that it did not enter. Not only were teachers and pastors driven from their stations, but the children of Masons were excluded from the schools, and members from their churches. The Sacrament was refused to Masons by formal vote of the Church, for no other offense than their Masonic connection. Families were divided. Brother was arrayed against brother, father against son, and even wives against their husbands. Desperate efforts were made to take away chartered rights from Masonic Corporations and to pass laws that would prevent Masons from holding their meetings and performing their ceremonies.

Popular feeling that Masons considered themselves above the law produced a public campaign against Freemasonry. It was claimed that their secrecy hid illegal and immoral activities, that Masonic oaths were unlawful and "bloody," and that Masons sought to subvert American political and religious institutions. Women joined the anti-Masonic movement by demanding that their husbands resign because of the exclusion of women from Masonry. Many Americans embraced what they called the "Blessed Spirit" of fighting to abolish Freemasonry.

This animosity quickly extended into politics. Among the prominent politicians who supported anti-Masonism were former president John Quincy Adams, William A. Seward (later a founder of the Republican Party and secretary of state during the Civil War), Daniel Webster, and Henry Clay, a former grand master of Kentucky. The firebrand of anti-

Masonry was Thurlow Weed, a New York journalist who hated President Andrew Jackson. Grabbing onto the Morgan matter as a weapon to use against Jackson, he cynically declared that the body, whether it was Morgan's or not, was "a good enough Morgan until after the election in the autumn."

The target of Weed's animosity and venom was born on March 15, 1767, at Waxhaw, South Carolina. Called "Andy" and "Old Hickory," Jackson became a soldier in the War for Independence at age thirteen. He and his brother, Robert (age sixteen), were captured by the British and mistreated, a fact that Jackson never forgot. When both he and his brother contracted smallpox, their mother obtained their release. Robert died two days later, and Andrew was sick for several weeks. In December 1784, Jackson left Waxhaw for Salisbury, North Carolina, and practiced law. Admitted to the North Carolina bar in 1787, he became the U.S. attorney for the Southwest Territory in 1790.

The exact date on which Jackson was made a Mason is not known. The Masonic journal *The Builder* stated in 1925: "The claim of Greeneville Lodge No. 3 of Tenn. (formerly No. 43 of N.C.) seems to be the most weighty. An original transcript of the lodge record for Sept. 5, 1801 shows that he [Jackson] was a member at the time."

Several other sources cited different lodges in Tennessee and North Carolina as claiming Jackson as a member or as attending, including two Nashville lodges (Harmony Lodge No. 1 as early as 1801 and Cumberland Lodge No. 8 in 1805) and Tennessee Lodge No. 2 in Knoxville. *The Builder* said that possibly he was made a Mason at one of the Nashville lodges, "since he came to that city at the age of 21, but the record is not clear." It is certain from records that he took an active interest in Freemasonry at an early age and throughout his life.

A man of his times, with a hot temper, Jackson often engaged in duels. Among his opponents were Governor John Sevier and Charles Dickinson. Jackson took a bullet to the chest and carried it in his body the rest of his life. Many of the duels resulted from insults to Rachel.

In 1812, Jackson became commander of the Tennessee militia and major general of a group of volunteers. Among them was Sam Houston, later to be a member of the Cumberland Lodge No. 8, a congressman from Tennessee, the governor of Tennessee, a Texas revolutionary, the president of Republic of Texas, and the governor of Texas. Another volunteer under Jackson was Davy Crockett, a Freemason who would garner fame as a frontiersman, a colorful member of Congress, and a defender of the Alamo. Volunteer Thomas Claiborne later became the first Grand Master of Masons in Tennessee.

An interesting footnote in the War of 1812 is that the author of the words of "The Star-Spangled Banner," Francis Scott Key, was a Freemason. The tune "To Anacreon in Heaven" that was eventually to be the music for Key's poem was composed by an English Freemason named John Stafford Smith. He was a member of Inverness Lodge No. 4, London. The first use of the melody is not known, but it was noted as being played in a Masonic orphanage in Ireland. It became a popular drinking song in British pubs.

As Freemasons John Paul Jones gave the U.S. Navy its motto "I have not yet begun to fight" in the Revolutionary War, a seagoing Mason who became a hero of the War in 1812 had coined an equally rousing, patriotic nautical battle cry. Recounting the story of James Lawrence in the California publication *Scottish Rite Journal of Freemasonry*, the Masonic scholar John E. Lindsey began by depicting the fifty-cannon U.S. frigate *Chesapeake* sailing into Boston Harbor in 1813 to replace its ill captain. His replacement was a "young, brilliant officer" who had been hailed as a national hero because of a long record of victories at sea and happened to be in Boston at that time.

Reluctantly accepting command of the *Chesapeake* on May 18, 1813, James Lawrence selected "a capable man, Augustus Ludlow," a native of Delaware and a Mason, as his first lieutenant. They faced the fifty-two-gun British frigate *Shannon*. Commanded by Sir Philip Broke, it blockaded Boston Harbor. Broke sent taunting messages to Lawrence to leave the harbor and meet him in a duel on the open sea.

"Before this battle," Lindsey writes, "Lawrence's record was a textbook example of professional skill, cunning, and courage. He entered the navy as a midshipman in 1798 and was commissioned Lieutenant in 1802." Assigned to the *Enterprise,* he sailed to Tripoli to join the squadron of Commodore Edward Preble, headquartered at Malta.

Regarded as the center of the Tripolitan War (1801–1805), it's known to most Americans from the stirring "to the shores of Tripoli" in the anthem of the U.S. Marine Corps.

The seaport had been a haven for Mediterranean Sea pirates who constantly blackmailed England, France, the United States, and other nations that conducted merchant business in that region. Commanding a gunboat when the U.S. frigate *Philadelphia* struck and became trapped on an uncharted ledge while pursuing a Moorish pirate ship into the harbor, Lawrence was made second in command in the boldest and most daring exploit of the war. Commodore Preble assigned Stephen Decatur Jr. to take a ketch, slip into the harbor at night, and burn the *Philadelphia* to prevent it from being used to block the harbor. On February 15, 1804, seventy-four volunteers, including Lawrence, reached the *Philadelphia,* sprang aboard, expelled the crew, and set it on fire. They then fled under fire from the shore batteries and pursuing Tripolitan vessels and escaped unharmed while the *Philadelphia* burned and sank. Lawrence served on the Barbary coast for five years and became the first lieutenant aboard the *Constitution.* Known as "Old Ironsides," it was Preble's flagship. Lawrence was then promoted and given the command of the *Argus,* the *Vixen,* and the *Wasp.* As master commandant of the *Hornet* in the War of 1812, he cruised the Brazilian coast to curtail Britain's use of ports.

"With abundant experience in nighttime maneuvers," Lindsey writes, "Lawrence evaded the ship under cover of darkness and escaped within firing range of the English sloop-of-war, *Peacock.* Lawrence's *Hornet* and the *Peacock* were evenly matched with 20 guns each. In eleven minutes the *Peacock* was sinking and surrendered."

Four month later (June 1, 1813), Lawrence sailed out of Boston on the *Chesapeake* to duel Sir Philip Broke's *Shannon* with an untrained and undisciplined crew. The ships began firing, but soon the *Chesapeake* began to flounder. She drifted helplessly astern and directly toward Broke's *Shannon.* Assembling a party to board the *Shannon* as soon as the vessels struck, Lawrence gave the order as a musket ball mortally wounded him. While his crewmen carried him below, he muttered the second most-famous order in the annals of the U.S. Navy: "Don't give up the ship!"

English sailors rushed onto *Chesapeake* and in fierce hand-to-hand fighting, *Chesapeake* had sixty-one killed and eighty-five wounded. Unable to sail, she was towed into Halifax, Nova Scotia, to be later turned into a British warship. Lawrence lived three days at Halifax and died on June 6, 1813. Buried with military honors by the British at Halifax, his remains were later returned to Salem, Massachusetts, and finally moved to Trinity Churchyard, New York City. He was buried with both grand lodge and military honors on September 16, 1813, two weeks before his thirty-second birthday. In *10,000 Famous Freemasons,* William R. Denslow writes, "Although it is known that Lawrence was a Mason, his lodge membership remains a mystery." The Grand Lodge of New York passed the following resolution: "Resolved that it be referred to the grand officers, that in case there should be a public funeral of our deceased brother, the late gallant Captain Lawrence, to take measures, if they should deem it proper, to assemble the lodges in this city (N.Y.) to join in the procession." The *Field Book of the War of 1812* states that Lawrence was buried with military and Masonic honors. A New York lodge chartered on May 18, 1814, was named in his honor.

Andrew Jackson, the most famous Mason of the War of 1812 to garner glory and fame, campaigned for president in 1824 on his popularity as a hero and received a plurality of popular votes in the election, but the House of Representatives chose John Quincy Adams as president. During the discussion before the selection of a president, he had refused to agree to appoint Henry Clay as secretary of state in exchange for Clay's support. In the next election (1828), Jackson received 68 percent of the electoral votes. In 1832, he won 76 percent in a contest with Clay (Past Grand Master of Kentucky) and with the candidate of the first "third party" in U.S. history.

The burgeoning anti-Freemason movement had given birth to the the Anti-Mason Party. It grew so powerful that its candidates were elected governor in Pennsylvania and in Vermont, to the U.S. Senate and House of Representatives, and to the legislatures in several states. In 1832, the party invented the national nominating convention. Meeting in Baltimore, the delegates chose William Wirt as its standard bearer for president. In a three-way contest against Jackson and Clay, Wirt carried only Vermont. As a direct result of the anti-mason movement, Masons became more of a social group than an intellectual society. The number of U.S. Masons declined from about 100,000 to 40,000 in ten years. New York went from 20,000 to 3,000 and from 480 to 82 lodges. Lodges in Vermont, Pennsylvania, Rhode Island Massachusetts, Connecticut, and Ohio ceased meeting. Officers resigned and new ones could not be found. For several years, there were no initiations.

The view of Freemasonry was that the Anti-Mason Party was organized "to put down the Masonic Institution as subversive of good government," but really for political aggrandizement of its leaders, "who used the opposition to Freemasonry merely as a stepping-stone to their own advancement to office." The anti-Freemasonry historian William L. Stone writes that "the fact is not to be disguised that anti-Masonry had become thoroughly political, and its spirit was vindictive towards the Freemasons without distinction as to guilt or innocence."

Albert G. Mackey's *Revised History of Freemasonry* states:

> Notwithstanding the opposition that from time to time has been exhibited to Freemasonry in every country, America is the only one where it assumed the form of a political party. This, however, may very justly be attributed to the peculiar nature of its popular institutions. Here the ballot-box is considered the most potent engine for the government of rulers as well as people, and is, therefore, resorted to in cases in which, in more despotic governments, the powers of the Church and State would be exercised.

The anti-Masonic convention itself declared, "The object of anti-Masonry, in nominating and electing candidates for Presidency and Vice-Presidency, is to deprive Masonry of the support which it derives from the power and patronage of the executive branch of the United States Government. To effect this object, will require that candidates besides possessing the talents and virtues requisite for such exalted stations be known as men decidedly opposed to secret societies." The Masonic view was that the Anti-Mason Party combined "religious fanatics and political opportunists" who "exercised a devastating effect on the Fraternity."

By early 1828, anti-Masonry was rampant in New York. An Empire State historian of Freemasonry notes that attendance at the Annual Communication of 1828 was "only slightly affected," with 30 lodges represented, as compared to 142 represented in the 2 grand lodges in 1825. During 1828 only three warrants for new lodges were issued. There were 103 suspensions on the basis of nonpayment of dues, compared to 38 suspensions in the combined lodges in 1825.

After 1828, the effects of anti-Masonry on individual Masons, local lodges, and the Grand Lodge of New York became even more apparent. Early in 1829 there was a strong movement to yield to public pressure to disband lodges. Ontario County Masons recommended to lodges and chapters in western New York "the expediency of returning their charters." Six lodges of Monroe County, including one in Rochester, surrendered their charters to the grand lodge in "acquiescence to public opinion." Refusing to give in, delegates from nineteen lodges in Cayuga and Onondaga counties held a meeting on May 5, 1829, and disclaimed all prior knowledge of "the Morgan affair" and denied all the charges made against the fraternity.

The lodges asserted, "We venerate Freemasonry for its antiquity, we admire it for its moral principles, and we love it for its charity benevolence." They formally resolved that "in the opinion of this convention it would be inexpedient and improper to take measures for the surrender of Masonic charters," and that "brethren be respectfully advised to adopt no measures in relation to that subject."

Records show that during the period of anti-Masonic "excitement" in New York, only 76 lodges, out of the 484 existent in 1825, surrendered their charters. But in the 1925 book *The Craft, Morgan and Anti-Masonry,* the Reverend John C. Palmer, the grand chaplain of the Grand Lodge of the District of Columbia, wrote:

The pressure was so strong that withdrawals by individuals and bodies were numerous. In 1827, two hundred and twenty-seven lodges were represented in the Grand Lodge of New York. In 1835, the number had dwindled to forty-one. Every lodge in the State of Vermont surrendered its Charter or became dormant; and the Grand Lodge, for several years, ceased to hold its sessions.

The Masonic Temple was left in twain; its brotherhood scattered, its [members] without work; its working tools shattered.

Thus Masonry endured the penalty of the mistaken zeal of those fearful brethren who thought that the revealing of the ritual to profane eyes would destroy the Order and who hoped to save it by removing the traitor within the camp.

By 1835, anti-Masonry as a political force dissipated as public debate shifted from suspicions of secret societies to the growing controversy over slavery. Ironically, the country that turned against Freemasonry would create several new "secret societies" that were modeled on Freemasonry. These included the Order of Odd Fellows, the Knights of Pythias, the Sons of Temperance, and the Roman Catholic Knights of Columbus.

The anti-Mason tide in New York began turning in 1836. In June, James Herring, the grand secretary, reported that anti-Masonry in the state was "rapidly dying out and revival of Masonic labors and usefulness begins to be manifest."

In one of the territories that would soon loom large in the question of slavery and saving the Union, a group of American Freemasons was about to enter the histories of Masonry and national folklore, legend, and myth. This handful of men had settled on land north of the Rio Grande that belonged to Mexico. Determined to wrest away the territory and see it eventually a part of the United States, they would become Masonic martyrs and American heroes by fighting a formidable Mexican army. They would be remembered in U.S. history in another patriotic battle cry by taking a stand to the last man in an old Spanish mission deep in the heart of Texas.

Chapter 8

The Masonic Republic of Texas

A TEXAS HISTORIAN WRITES THAT THE LONE STAR STATE AND "the Masons who shaped its course of history are so interwoven that they cannot be separated." Harry L. Haywood, another Masonic historian, proudly asserts, "Texas is truly the daughter of Masonry."

Texas Masons record that the first-known Mason to go to Texas was Zebulon Pike, in 1806. At that time, Americans were granted rights to settle in the territory claimed by Mexico, in which Masonry was well established among the educated classes of Mexican society. By the 1830s, Americans greatly outnumbered Texas Mexicans (Texicans). When Antonio López de Santa Anna, the Mexican leader, tried to reverse the trend by outlawing slavery and enforcing collection of customs duties, Americans rebelled. On October 25, 1828, the Mexican government banned Freemasonry in a region that included a vast part of the former Spanish empire north of the Rio Grande.

Seven years later (March 1835), five Master Masons met beneath an oak tree in Brazoria and petitioned Grand Master John H. Holland of Louisiana for a charter to form a lodge in the region they called Texas. On March 1, 1836, Sam Houston and fifty-eight other delegates rode into the town of Washington-on-the-Brazos for a convention to declare "Texican" independence. Twenty-two of the delegates were Masons. Eleven of a twenty-five-man committee to draw up a Constitution of the Republic were Masons. The Declaration was unanimously signed by men who knew that like the signers of 1776, they might be issuing their death warrants.

"From the Declaration of Independence and the Constitution to the event of lowering of the Texas flag and the raising of the Stars and Stripes," writes a historian, "Masons took most of the major parts."

The father of Freemasonry in Texas was Stephen Austin. Born in Virginia on November 3, 1793, and raised in southeastern Missouri, he attended school in Connecticut and graduated with distinction from Transylvania University in Kentucky. At age twenty he was elected to the territorial legislature of Missouri and was reelected to that position each year until 1819, when he moved to Arkansas. His father, Moses, received a grant of land in Texas for the purpose of colonization, but died soon after returning to Missouri from a trip to Texas. Bequeathed the grant, with an instruction to carry it to a successful completion, Austin encountered numerous delays and frustrations in dealing with the Mexican government before introducing a number of colonists from the United States. Described as "unassuming" with "a kindly presence," he is credited with achieving unparalleled influence over often unruly settlers in "Anglo Texas."

Masonic history records that he attempted to organize a Masonic lodge in 1828, when he and six other Masons met at San Felipe and petitioned the Grand York Lodge of Mexico for a charter dispensation. The petition evidently reached Mexico at the height of a quarrel between the "Yorkinos" and "Escoceses" (adherents of the Scottish Rite) and disappeared.

The convention appointed Sam Houston commander in chief of the Texas army of liberation. Born in Rockbridge County, Virginia, on March 2, 1793, Houston lost his father, moved to Tennessee with his family, and spent his early years with Cherokee Indians. He was adopted by a member of the tribe. After serving in the Thirty-ninth Infantry (July 1813–May 1818), he studied law at Nashville, practiced in Lebanon, and was twice elected to Congress. He earned Masonic degrees in Cumberland Lodge No. 8, Nashville, in 1817, but left the Cumberland Lodge on November 20, 1817, apparently accused of unspecified "un-Masonic conduct." In June 1821, he reaffiliated and is believed to have been a charter member of Nashville Lodge No. 37. He served as a junior warden and in 1824 attended a grand lodge as a past master

Elected governor of Tennessee in 1827, Houston fell into disfavor in part because of a mysterious marriage that lasted only a few weeks. Leaving the state, he made his way up the Arkansas to the mouth of the Illinois and lived for three years with his former Cherokee father-by-adoption. In 1832, he went to Texas. On March 6, 1836, as commander in chief of Texan rebel forces, he left Washington-on-the-Brazos to take command of his troops. Meanwhile, a small group of Texans had taken up a defensive position in a crumbling old Spanish mission that went by the name Alamo.

Founded in 1718, Mission San Antonio de Valero's purpose was winning the Indians to Christ. It was constructed by Indians under supervision of Spanish priests, but it was so poorly designed that the roof collapsed and the work was left uncompleted. By 1793, most Indians in the area had died from disease and San Antonio de Valero was closed. In 1803, a Spanish cavalry unit from Alamo de Parras, Mexico, quartered in it and gave it the name Pueblo del Alamo (House of Cottonwood).

In 1835 as the Texicans began their revolution, Santa Anna sent his brother-in-law, General Martin de Cos, to reinforce the Alamo. He made it into a fortress with cannons placed on the walls. In December 1835, a force of 400 Texans led by Ben Milam made their way to San Antonio to engage Cos in battle. After several days of fighting, he surrendered by raising a white flag and departed, leaving his cannons and promising not to return. Infuriated, Santa Anna decided to redeem his and Mexican honor by personally retaking the Alamo.

While Santa Anna prized the fortified old mission and was determined to reclaim it, Houston decided that it was too isolated and the better Texas military strategy was to let Santa Anna have it, but only after it was reduced to rubble. To carry out the policy, he sent Colonel James "Jim" Bowie, a fellow Tennessee Masonic brother, and thirty compatriots to do the deed. Although Bowie was born in Tennessee in 1795, he'd grown up in the bayou country of Louisiana. Famed as an alligator wrestler, Indian fighter, and duelist, he was declared by Henry Clay, one of America's most prominent politicians from Kentucky, as "the greatest fighter in the Southwest." This burst of admiration was the result of Clay having witnessed a demonstration of Bowie's courage and chivalry in 1832. Clay was traveling with Bowie and a young woman on a stagecoach when another passenger lit "an obnoxious pipe." After he ignored the lady's plea that he desist, Bowie persuaded him to comply by drawing a very large knife that became Bowie's namesake trademark. A report of this event and other colorful Bowie episodes, including his role at the Alamo, caused the British historian Thomas Carlyle to exclaim, "By Hercules! The man is greater than Caesar! The Texans ought to build him a monument."

Records of Bowie's Freemasonry and membership in Louisiana's Humble Cottage Lodge No. 19 were destroyed in a fire in 1850, thirty years after he arrived in San Antonio, Texas, and married the beautiful daughter of the vice governor of Coahulla, Mexico, and Mexican Texas. She and their two children died in a cholera epidemic in 1830.

"After arriving in San Antonio," notes a Texan historian, "somehow Bowie couldn't bring himself to destroy the old mission." Hearing that Santa Anna was marching toward the Alamo, he became even more determined to save it. On February 2, 1836, he wrote, "We will rather die in these ditches than give them up."

After Bowie and his men decided not to raze the Alamo, but defend it, command of the makeshift fortress was given to William Barret Travis. Born in August 1809, he was a lawyer in Alabama and began a newspaper, the *Claiborne Herald*. He joined the Masonic order at Alabama Lodge No. 3 and accepted a position as adjutant of the Twenty-sixth Regiment, Eighth Brigade, Fourth Division of the Alabama Militia. A year later, he abandoned his wife, son, and unborn daughter and departed for Texas, probably because he suspected his wife of infidelity, doubted the parenthood of their unborn child, and killed a man because of it. He arrived in Texas early in 1831, after the Law of April 6, 1830, which made such immigration illegal. At San Felipe de Austin on May 21, 1831, he obtained land from Stephen Austin, listed his marital status as single, and opened a law practice in Anahuac on the eastern end of Galveston Bay. He moved his legal practice to San Felipe and met Rebecca Cummings. His first wife began divorce proceedings in 1834, charging him with desertion. Travis may not have known when the divorce became final, because he was embroiled in the rapidly moving events of the Texas revolution.

In late June 1835, Travis led about twenty-five men by way of Harrisburg and Galveston Bay in an amphibious assault on the Gonzales, a Mexican position, and captured it. When General Cos set up command at San Antonio, he branded Travis and the others outlaws and demanded that they be turned over for military trial. When Cos demanded the surrender of the Gonzales in October 1835, Travis joined the hundreds of Texans who rallied to its defense, but arrived too late to take part in the action. He remained with the militia and accompanied it to the Alamo.

When Bowie arrived with 100 volunteers, he and Travis quarreled over command, but Bowie fell ill after an injury from a fall that forced him to bed. Directing the preparation for defending the Alamo against the anticipated arrival of Santa Anna and the main command of the Mexican army, Travis and the engineer Green B. Jameson strengthened the walls by constructing palisades to fill in the gaps, mounting cannons, and storing provisions. Travis wrote letters asking for reinforcements, but only thirty-five men came from the Gonzales, raising the number of the Alamo's defenders to approximately 183.

Riding to the Alamo to bolster Travis's force was a burly frontiersman from Tennessee by way of three terms in the U.S. House of Representatives. His figure would become large in the history, lore, and legend of the U.S. frontier and saga of Texan freedom and overshadow the besieged defenders of the Alamo. A future American icon and already a legend in his own time, David Crockett was born on August 17, 1786, in northwestern Tennessee. Able to shoot out a candle at 100 yards, "Davy" was reputed to have killed 105 bears in a single season, a few of them with a knife. After losing his House seat in 1835, he told his constituents, "You can all go to hell. I'm goin' to Texas."

Because the Masonic lodge in Weakley County, Tennessee, was burned during the Civil War, the only proof that Crockett was a Mason is a ceremonial Masonic apron that was made for him by Mrs. A. C. Massie of Washington, D.C., when he was in Congress.

On February 24, Travis addressed a letter "To the People of Texas and All Americans in the World" that justified the Texan struggle for independence. By then, Santa Anna's advance force had arrived in San Antonio. During the period of preparation, Travis had sent James Butler Bonham, an old friend, classmate, and fellow lawyer, to ride to meet with Colonel James Fannin at Goliad and appeal to him to leave Goliad to reinforce the Alamo. Born in Red Banks, South Carolina, on February 20, 1807, Bonham gained military experience as a colonel of artillery in the Alabama militia's "Mobile Grays." As a lieutenant in Houston's army, he'd arrived at the Alamo with Bowie on January 17, 1836. When Fannin refused the appeal to abandon Goliad, Bonham returned to the Alamo under heavy Mexican fire and was the last person to enter the mission before Santa Anna launched his all-out attack.

A demand for surrender from Santa Anna was answered by a cannon shot, ignited by Travis. When Santa Anna decided his forces were ready, he ordered an assault on the Alamo just before dawn on March 6, 1836. The Mexicans overpowered the Texans within a few hours. Travis died early in the battle from a single bullet in the head. His body and those of the other defenders were burned. At that moment, the Alamo and its defenders gained a status in American patriotic fact and legend, and American Masonic history, alongside Lexington, Concord, Bunker Hill, and numerous other battles of the Revolution, sailors and Marines at Tripoli, and Jackson at New Orleans.

In a chronicle of Texas Freemasonry, the fight for the Alamo unfolded this way:

> Unsheathing his sword during a lull in the virtually incessant bombardment Colonel William Barret Travis drew a line on the ground before his battle-weary men. In a voice trembling with emotion he described the hopelessness of their plight and said, "those prepared to give their lives in freedom's cause, come over to me."
>
> Without hesitation, every man, save one, crossed the line, Colonel James Bowie, stricken with pneumonia, asked that his cot be carried over.

For twelve days now, since February 23, when Travis answered Mexican General Antonio Lopez de Santa Anna's surrender ultimatum with a cannon shot, the defenders had withstood the onslaught of an army which ultimately numbered 4,000 men. Committed to death inside the Alamo were 189 known patriots who valued freedom more than life itself. Many, such as the 32 men and boys from Gonzales [Texas] who made their way through the Mexican lines in answer to Travis's plea for reinforcements, were colonists. Theirs was a fight against Santa Anna's intolerable decrees. Others were volunteers such as David Crockett and his "Tennessee Boys" who owned nothing in Texas, and owned nothing to it. Theirs was a fight against tyranny wherever it might be. A handful were native Texans of Spanish and Mexican descent who suffered under the same injustices as the other colonists.

With ammunition and supplies all but exhausted, yet determined to make a Mexican victory more costly than a defeat, those who rallied to Texas awaited the inevitable. In the chilly, predawn hours of March 6, with bugles sounding the dreaded "Deguello" (meaning give no quarter), columns of Mexican soldiers attacked from the north, east, south, and west. Twice repulsed by withering musket fire and cannon shot, they concentrated their third attack at the battered north wall.

Travis, with a single shot through his forehead, fell across his cannon. The Mexicans swarmed through the breach and into the plaza. At frightful cost they fought their way to the Long Barrack and blasted its massive doors with cannon shot. Its defenders, asking no quarter and receiving none, were put to death with grapeshot, musket fire and bayonets.

Crockett, using his rifle as a club, fell as the attackers, now joined by reinforcements who stormed the south wall, turned to the chapel. The Texans inside soon suffered the fate of their comrades. Bowie, his pistols emptied, his famous knife bloodied, and his body riddled, died on his cot.

Santa Anna had lost nearly 600 men, but said, "It was but a small affair." One of his officers, Colonel Juan Almonte, is said to have muttered,
"Another such victory and we are ruined." Three weeks later at Goliad,
Santa Anna coldly ordered the massacre of more than 300 prisoners
taken at the Battle of Coleto Creek.

After the fall of the Alamo, Houston and Secretary of War Thomas J.
Rusk led a small force eastward and arrived at Buffalo Bayou, a few
miles southeast of the present-day city that honors Houston with its
name. On the morning of April 19, they crossed to within half a mile of
the mouth of the San Jacinto River. On April 21, they prepared to make
a surprise attack on an outnumbering army of Mexicans under General
Santa Anna. Houston wrote:

> This morning we are in preparation to meet Santa Anna. It is the
> only chance of saving Texas. From time to time I have looked for re-
> inforcements in vain. We will only have about 700 men to march
> with. We go to conquer. It is wisdom growing out of necessity to
> meet the enemy. Now every consideration enforces it. The troops
> are in fine spirits and now is the time for action. We shall use our
> best efforts to fight the enemy to such advantage as will insure vic-
> tory though the odds, are greatly against us. I leave the result in the
> hands of a wise God, and rely upon his providence. My country will
> do justice to those who serve her. The rights for which we fight
> will be secure and Texas Free!

Arrayed on the battle line were regiments under Sidney Sherman, artillery under George W. Hockley, infantry under Henry Millard, and calvary under Mirabeau B. Lamar. Houston led the infantry charge to the
sound of the battle cries "Remember the Alamo!" and "Remember
Goliad!"

Taken by surprise, the Mexicans rallied briefly, turned, fled, and were
mauled by the attacking Texans. Santa Anna attempted to escape, but
his horse bogged down in a bayou. The next day, Texans looking for
stragglers found him without realizing his identity until other prisoners
addressed him as "El Presidente." He was promptly escorted to Houston.

At this point, according to William R. Denslow in *10,000 Famous Freemasons,* Santa Anna gave the Masonic sign of distress, first to James A. Sylvester, then to Houston. Bound by the tenets of the Craft, Houston was compelled to spare "Brother" Santa Anna's life

The Masonic scholar James David Carter writes of this event in *Masonry in Texas: Background, History, and Influence to 1846,* "It may be that Masons saved the life of Santa Anna but if so, they did not act because he made claim to their mercy as Masons. All of the Masons to whom he appealed knew that Santa Anna disowned Masonry; that further, his many offenses against Texas and Mexican Masons had placed him outside the protection of any Masonic obligation. Santa Anna was saved because the Texas leaders considered him worth more to Texas alive than dead."

Houston may have calculated that his victory was tenuous at best and that to execute Santa Anna might enshroud him with a martyrdom he didn't deserve. By sparing him, Houston burnished his own memory, not only as a liberator and champion of freedom but also as a humanitarian who lived by the principles of Freemasonry.

He was elected the first president of the Republic of Texas on October 22, 1836, receiving 4,374 of the total 5,104 votes. His term expired on December 12, 1838, but he served again as president (December 12, 1841–December 9, 1844) while Texans strove for admission of Texas to the Union. This was achieved on December 29, 1845. In March 1846, Houston was elected to the U.S. Senate and served until 1859. He was elected governor of the state of Texas (1859–1861) and retired from public affairs. During this period, he affiliated with Holland Lodge No. 36 of Louisiana, which became Holland Lodge No. 1 of Texas. On December 20, 1837, he presided over a meeting that established the Grand Lodge of Texas.

Leaving Holland Lodge on July 14, 1842, Houston was next reported as a member of Forest Lodge No. 19, Huntsville, Texas, in 1851. He was knighted in Commandery No. 1, Washington, D.C., on February 23, 1853. He died at Huntsville, Texas, on July 26, 1863.

Every president and vice president of the Republic of Texas was a Mason, as was every chief justice of the republic. Fifteen Masons were in the first House of Representatives, seven in the first senate, and eleven in the executive branch. Thirty-one Texas governors were Masons. Two served as grand masters. The last president of Texas watched the lowering of the Lone Star flag and the hoisting of the Stars and Stripes of the United States on February 19, 1846.

Stephen Austin, "the Father of Texas," did not live to see the formation of the grand lodge. He'd died on December 27, 1836. At a celebration of the Festival of St. John the Baptist (Masonry's patron saint) in 1844 at Portland, Maine, George K. Teulon, a member of the Grand Lodge of Texas, in reply to a toast to "the Freemasons of the Republic," asserted, "Texas is emphatically a Masonic country. Our national emblem, the Lone Star, was chosen from the emblems selected by Freemasonry to illustrate the moral virtues. It is a five-pointed star, and alludes to the five points of fellowship." A Texan Masonic history boasts:

> We can be proud of our Masonic heritage and our involvement in the history of Texas. Proud of the men who died at Velasco, Goliad, the Grass Fight, Coleto and San Jacinto. Proud of Masons who led the men those thirteen days at the Alamo and bought time for Brother Sam Houston to strengthen the Texas army for the defeat of Santa Anna at San Jacinto. Houston's army attacked Santa Anna's Mexican army and defeated a force nearly twice its size in only eighteen minutes. Proud of the many Masons in the government of the Republic. Long may we remember their names and their deeds and their actions.

The Alamo gave Texas heroic martyrs. The victory at San Jacinto cleared the way to Texas freedom, its eventual admission to the Union, and the advancement of the doctrine of manifest destiny that would make the United States the continental nation that had been a dream of the Founding Fathers.

Chapter 9

Blood Brothers: Rebs and Yankees

A DECADE AFTER TEXANS WRESTED A COUNTRY FROM MEXICO, the fourth president of the United States to embrace Freemasonry set his eyes and heart on obtaining a large portion of the former Spanish empire adjoining Texas that still belonged to Mexico. James K. Polk planned to do this by grabbing New Mexico, Arizona, and California through negotiations if possible, but through force if necessary, whether Congress approved or not.

In one of the many strange quirks that litter the pages of history books and make their way into crossword puzzles, trivia games, and television quiz shows, the U.S. ambassador to the government of Mexico that succeeded General Antonio Lopez de Santa Anna is best known for the fact that his name is associated with yuletide decoration. A Christian Freemason and worldwide traveler, Joel Poinsett brought to Mexico the York Rite that Mexicans called "Yorquino." A Charleston, South Carolina, aristocrat and inveterate sojourner, he paid an initial visit to Mexico in the summer of 1822. He met and formed an unfavorable opinion of then emperor Iturbide. He took a post that had been originally offered to Andrew Jackson at a time when the U.S. government was predominantly Protestant and the democratic United States was suspicious of its Catholic and aristocratic neighbor to the south, concerned by the increasing British presence in Mexico, and alarmed about Mexican intentions in Cuba.

Poinsett was to "represent democracy" and support the Monroe Doctrine, which was intended to keep Europe from further intrusion into the American hemisphere. Historians interpret this in the case of Mexico as a means of blunting Mexican tendency to seek European affiliations in trade. The new ambassador went to Mexico City to present "complaints of his fellow-citizens against bewildering commercial regulations; to oppose Mexico's cherished designs regarding Cuba," and to acquire territory when the mere suggestion of such a transaction confirmed suspicions among Mexicans regarding the United States, which "wounded Mexican pride, and intensified Mexican irritation." To accomplish these ambitious goals, Poinsett believed that he had to "change the attitudes of the Mexican government" by challenging the Spanish born who still looked toward Europe. Although Poinsett was a Freemason, many of those who opposed him were Scottish Rite Masons who resented that in 1824 he'd arranged for five lodges to be chartered by the Grand Lodge of New York, all of which would work in the York Rite. The next year, these lodges formed a York Rite Grand Lodge for Mexico (La Gran Logia Nacional Mexicana) that grew to more than 100 lodges.

In the interim, Iturbide's empire came to an end (1823) as the result of a civil war over the question of whether the country should be a centralized and conservative republic, or a federal and liberal one. Scottish Masons favored the republic, Yorquinos didn't. This conflict had thwarted Stephen Austin's desire to create lodges. The consequence of the warring Masons was a ban in 1828 of all secret societies that was enforced by police, who closed lodges that didn't obey.

When Poinsett left Mexico in January 1830, the York cause was collapsing and many other Yorquinos were fleeing the country. Both Scottish and York Freemasonry became largely dormant while the new Mexican National Rite rose to prominence. Mexican Masonry embraced a degree system authored by Albert Pike, an American Masonic revolutionary, creator of modern U.S. Masonry, and brother of Zebulon Pike.

During Poinsett's term as ambassador in Mexico City, relations between Mexico and the United States would be settled by American soldiers acting on orders from President Polk. Born in Mecklenburg County, North Carolina, on November 2, 1795, he graduated with honors in 1818 from the University of North Carolina. As a young lawyer, he entered politics and served in the Tennessee legislature and became a friend and protégé of Andrew Jackson. Polk was initiated in Columbia Lodge No. 31, Columbia, Tennessee, on June 5, 1820. In 1825, he was exalted a Royal Arch Mason in LaFayette Chapter No. 4, Columbia. He served as the governor of Tennessee from 1839 through 1841 and was elected president of the United States in 1842.

When Mexican leaders threatened to invade Texas and take it back, the still fledgling Republic of Texas and the United States agreed that the United States would put troops on Texas soil as soon as Texas was accepted into the Union. In late August 1845, Brigadier General Zachary Taylor (nicknamed "Old Rough and Ready") and his troops were in place at Corpus Christi, with more soldiers arriving almost daily to bolster Taylor's "Army of Occupation."

A believer in Manifest Destiny, Polk despatched a diplomat to peacefully and amicably resolve the potentially explosive situation, but to U.S. advantage. Besides the question of whether Texas was free to join the Union, there were numerous unpaid claims against the Mexican government by private U.S. citizens. Exercising discretion granted to him by the secretary of war at Polk's direction, General Taylor held his troops in Corpus Christi in the hope Mexico would not move deeper into the Nueces Strip, a thinly populated territory lying between the Rio Nueces on the north and the Rio Grande on the south.

The diplomat, John Slidell, arrived in Mexico, only to find that a government that was in political turmoil refused to receive him. While Slidell was attempting to carry out his mission, the moderate government was overthrown by the militant Manuel Paredes. On January 13, 1846, Slidell decided that negotiations were no longer possible and instructed Taylor, through the secretary of war, to take a defensive position on the north bank of the Rio Grande. Taylor and his men left Corpus Christi and moved into the Lower Rio Grande Valley, set up a supply depot at Point Isabel, and constructed an earthen fieldwork opposite Matamoros. Francisco Mejia, the Mexican military commander, demanded that the Americans withdraw.

Old Rough and Ready not only refused but also informed Mejia that he had been sent there by the president of the United States. Unless and until Polk directed him to leave, he intended to stay put. He also pointed out to the Mexicans that he had not taken any hostile action, although the Mexican government had claimed that the mere presence of American troops was a hostile act. If war began, he warned, the responsibility for it would lie with whoever fired the first shot, something he and his troops "did not intend to do." What the Mexicans soon learned was that he had asked the U.S. Navy to blockade the mouth of the Rio Grande.

Resorting to psychological warfare, the Mexicans circulated letters in the American camp that were openly addressed to "foreign-born soldiers" of the U.S. army and that encouraged them to desert. This was a blatant appeal to Roman Catholics (particularly Irish) to come to the aid of a fellow Catholic country. When some troops (Catholic and Protestants) swam the river, Taylor ordered pickets to shoot on sight any U.S. soldier heading for the south bank of the Rio Grande. After at least two were killed, desertions declined. Throughout April 1846 a tension mounted along the border, the Mexican government sent Pedro Ampudia to head the Mexican forces at Matamoros. He was soon replaced by Mariano Arista. By then, the number of Mexican troops at Matamoros greatly increased. By the end of the month, Arista had more than 6,000 men, twice the number behind American earthworks that were now named "Fort Texas."

On April 24, 1846, Arista sent Taylor a letter making it clear that it was only a matter of time before the forces under his command would cross over the Rio Grande and attack Taylor's Army of Occupation. Old Rough and Ready lived up to his name. When Arista kept his promise, a war commenced.

President Polk exclaimed, "After reiterated menaces, Mexico has passed the boundary of the United States, has invaded our territory and shed American blood upon the American Soil. She has proclaimed that hostilities have commenced, and that the two nations are at war."

While Polk's motivation is generally attributed to a desire to advance Manifest Destiny, the historian Sanford H. Montaigne, the author of *Blood over Texas,* connects what is known as "the Mexican War" to a result of the Texas War for Independence and other factors. He posits theories that a "slave power" conspiracy existed in which a "slaveocracy" in the southern states stirred up the war to acquire more land for slavery, that western states wanted to add more territory to their political and economic power, that commercial groups in the United States desired ports and waterways on the Pacific, and that Mexico wanted a war with the United States for reasons related to national pride and political tranquility.

Fifteen years after the end of the war, generals, junior officers of all ranks, and enlisted men who were Masonic brothers would find themselves fighting each other in the U.S. Civil War. By 1861, there were thirty-eight grand lodges operating in the United States. Each was independent and absolutely sovereign within its own jurisdictional boundaries. This lack of a national leadership is a major reason why Freemasonry as a whole did not fracture along geographical boundaries, as did many of the other organizations on the eve of war. In those cases, groups such as the Baptist and Presbyterian churches and others all had some sort of national leadership council, comprised of representatives of all the various regions of the country. As war fractured the country, it splintered the national committees of many groups. Because there was no "Grand Lodge of America," individual lodges were on their own. This did not mean that Masons didn't feel the pain of division. In a letter drafted in June 1861, the Grand Lodge of Pennsylvania replied to a letter from the Grand Lodge of Tennessee:

> As to the present deplorable state of this country, Masons cannot fail to have opinions as to the cause that produced it. It is to be feared that some of our brethren are in arms against the union of the States; others are in the ranks of its defenders. Taught by the history of the Order... they have carried these principles into the formation of opinions on the present crisis in our national history. But while Masons, as individuals, have been thus influenced and are acting in harmony with such views, Freemasonry is a silent, unimpassioned, abstracted observer of events.
>
> Brethren, we, with you, deplore the present unnatural and deeply distressing condition of our national affairs.... But if this whirlwind threatens to overwhelm us, yet in this last extremity, the still small voice of Masonic faith will be uttered and heard, saying, "Brethren,

there is help at hand in this time of need. Surely your God is our God; your faith our faith; your landmarks our landmarks; your joy our joy; your prosperity our satisfaction." Then let us unitedly work together for the preservation and perpetuity of a common inheritance.... We will aid in maintaining unity, peace and concord, among the brethren and citizens of united sovereign States in our glorious Union. If all bonds should be broken, all ties rent asunder; if discord, dissension, and disruption, shall mark the decline and fall of the most wise and wonderful of the governments of mankind, let the Masonic temple, in all States, kingdoms, lands, peoples or confederacies, be common refuge of an indestructible Masonic fraternity.

Allen E. Roberts notes in *House Divided: The Story of Freemasonry and the Civil War* that while the war raged around them, Freemasons held on to "the ties and the idealism that brought them together in the first place." Thousands of Masons fought in the war. Many died, but the tenets of the Craft were able to overcome the animosity the war generated. Historians of the Craft cite a number of reasons for this, beginning with beliefs and tenets of the lodge that predated not only the Civil War but also the Constitution, the discovery of the New World, and, according to some, even the birth of Christ. A second reason given to explain why Masonry held together is that membership in a Masonic lodge was by choice. No man had ever been recruited into joining a lodge. Rules prohibited Masons from recruiting. A man who was interested in becoming a Mason must "of his own free will and accord" actively seek out a member of the lodge that he wished to join and ask him for a petition for membership. The third reason lay in structure of the Craft. Internal rules and customs helped the lodge as a whole avoid the turbulent politics and divisiveness of the war, allowing the lodge to continue to function as a place a man could go when he needed help or a quiet haven from the storms that raged outside the Craft.

The most famous example of these ties of brotherhood occurred at the Battle of Gettysburg. A turning point of the war, the battle resulted in more than 35,000 killed or wounded in the three days of fighting from July 1 to 3, 1863. Of those who fought, 17,930 were Freemasons, with roughly 5,600 of them being casualties. In a Confederate infantry attack known as Pickett's Charge, Major General George Pickett, a member of Dove Lodge No. 51, Richmond, Virginia, led nearly 12,000 men on a long rush across open fields toward the center of the Union line on Cemetery Ridge. One of the leaders of the charge, Brigadier General Lewis Addison Armistead, belonged to Alexandria-Washington Masonic Lodge No. 22, Alexandria, Virginia. Originally from North Carolina, he had attended West Point and served in the U.S. Army for a number of years before resigning his commission to fight for the Confederacy. During that time, he had occasion to serve with Winfield Scott Hancock of Charity Lodge No. 190, Norristown, Pennsylvania, while both men were in the West. The two became good friends. After Armistead's resignation, it had been nearly two and a half years since the two men had any contact.

At Gettysburg, Hancock, now a major general, was in command of Union troops on Cemetery Ridge on July 1. He organized them into a front that withstood three days of pounding by Confederate guns. On July 3, his troops were in the center of the Union line and the focus of Pickett's Charge. During the fight, Armistead was shot from his horse and mortally wounded. Hancock's saddle was struck, driving nails and pieces of wood into his thigh. Armistead exhibited the Masonic sign of distress that was recognized by Captain Henry Harrison Bingham, the judge-advocate of Hancock's Second Corps and member of Chartiers Lodge No. 297, Canonsburg, Pennsylvania. Rushing to Armistead, he declared he was a Mason.

As the two men spoke, Armistead realized that Bingham had direct access to Hancock. He gave him personal effects, including his Masonic watch and the Bible on which he had taken his Masonic obligations. Bingham returned to the Union camp to deliver the items to Hancock. Armistead died two days later.

In Galveston, a Confederate major named Tucker performed Masonic funeral services for a Union captain named Wainwright who had died in Tucker's prison. In a public procession consisting of Union and Confederate soldiers, wearing the insignia of the order, and accompanied by a proper military escort, Wainwright's body was taken to the Episcopal cemetery. In another case, a Masonic Union naval commander named Hart was killed on board his vessel during a lengthy bombardment. A small craft sailed into the Louisiana port under a truce flag and asked for a Mason. W. W. Leake responded by immediately opening a lodge to give Hart full Masonic rites.

Some Masons wore signs and symbols of the Craft on their uniforms, in the hope that a Mason on the other side would recognize him as a brother and spare him harm. Masons were also active in hospitals and care units at the sites of major battles. Hospitals were located on the farms or in the buildings owned by Masons. The Masonic Temple in Vicksburg was used as a hospital first by the Confederates, and later by the Union after the fall of Vicksburg.

Other Freemasons who played significant roles at the Battle of Gettysburg include:

Colonel Joshua Lawrence Chamberlain, United Lodge No. 8, Brunswick, Maine, was awarded the Congressional Medal of Honor for heroics on Little Round Top.

Captain Henry H. Bingham, Chartiers Lodge No. 297, Canonsburg, Pennsylvania, a life member of Union Lodge No. 121, Philadelphia. He received the Medal of Honor and was elected to Congress in 1878 and served thirty-three years.

Brigadier General John B. Gordon of Upson County, Georgia, attended the University of Georgia and trained in law. At the Battle of Antietam he was wounded so severely in the head that only a bullet hole in his hat prevented him from drowning in his own blood. He was wounded eight times. After the war, he was elected U.S. senator from Georgia three times and later governor of Georgia. Some publications listed him a member of Gate City Lodge No. 2, Atlanta, but members of the lodge say there are no records to support this claim.

Major General Henry Heth, senior warden of Rocky Mountain Lodge No. 205, Utah Territory. A close friend of Robert E. Lee, he was severely wounded at Gettysburg but survived.

Brigadier General Alfred Iverson, Columbian Lodge No. 108, Columbus, Georgia. His father was a U.S. senator from Georgia before the war.

Brigadier General Solomon Meredith, commander of the "Iron Brigade," also called the "Black Hat Brigade," had three sons in the Union army, two of whom were killed. He was a member of Cambridge Lodge No. 105, Indianapolis, Indiana.

Major General Carl Schurz, born in Cologne, Prussia, left Europe after supporting failed revolutions. A prominent politician, he backed Abraham Lincoln in the 1860 election. Given a general-ship to command the large number of Germans in the Union army, he did not enjoy a distinguished career in the Civil War. After the conflict, he served as an ambassador to Spain, U.S. senator from Missouri, and secretary of the interior. He died in 1906 in New York City, where a park is now named for him. He was a member of Herman Lodge No. 125, Philadelphia.

Brigadier General George T. "Tige" Anderson left college in Georgia to enter the Mexican War. Severely wounded in Gettysburg, he was a Freemason, but details of his membership are not known.

Brigadier General John H. H. Ward of New York City fought in many Civil War battles, but was removed from the army in 1864 for misbehavior and intoxication in the face of the enemy. This was disputed for thirty years and never settled. After the war, he served as a clerk of courts in New York. In 1903 while vaca-tioning in Monroe, New York, he was run over by a train and killed. He was a Mason in Metropolitan Lodge No. 273, New York City.

Other Masons at Gettysburg were:

Brigadier General Rufus Ingalls—Williamette Lodge No. 2, Oregon
Brigadier General Joseph B. Kershaw—Kershaw Lodge No. 29, South Carolina
Brigadier General Alfred T. A. Torbert—Temple Chapter No. 2, Delaware

Brigadier General William Barksdale—Columbus Lodge No. 5,
  Columbus, Mississippi
Major General David B. Birney—Franklin Lodge No. 134,
  Pennsylvania
Brigadier General Harry T. Hays—Louisiana Lodge No. 102,
  Louisiana
Major General Daniel Butterfield—Metropolitan Lodge No. 273,
  New York
Brigadier General John W. Geary—Philanthropy Lodge No. 255,
  Pennsylvania
Major General Alfred Pleasonton—Franklin Lodge No. 134,
  Pennsylvania
Brigadier General George J. Stannard—Franklin Lodge No. 4,
  Vermont
Brigadier General James L. Kemper—Linn Banks Lodge No. 126,
  Virginia
Major General George E. Pickett—Dove Lodge No. 51, Virginia
Brigadier General John D. Imboden—Staunton Lodge No. 13,
  Virginia

In 1993, the Grand Lodge of Pennsylvania completed and dedicated a monument on the Gettsyburg National Cemetery. It depicts "Brother Bingham, a Union officer, assisting Brother Armistead." The statue is called "Masonic Friend to Friend Masonic Memorial." In the words of Sheldon A. Munn, one of the Freemasons who helped bring about its construction, the monument is meant to "demonstrate to the world that Freemasonry is, indeed, a unique fraternity; that its bonds of friendship, compassion and brotherly love withstood the ultimate test during the most tragic and decisive period of our nation's history; it stood then as it stands now, as 'A Brotherhood Undivided!'"

Abraham Lincoln was not a Mason, but the Masonic historian Paul Bessel notes that "he possessed and displayed all the important qualities of Freemasonry: faith, hope, and charity, belief in God, the equality of all people, and the ability of each person to improve." He also "came into contact with many Masons." When the Grand Lodge of Illinois recessed a meeting being held during the 1860 presidential campaign, it called on Lincoln. He was reported to have said, "Gentlemen, I have always entertained a profound respect for the Masonic fraternity and have long cherished a desire to become a member."

When a Mason told Lincoln during the campaign that all his opponents were Freemasons, especially noting that Stephen A. Douglas was an early member of the Masonic lodge in Lincoln's home town of Springfield, Illinois, and asked why Lincoln was not, Lincoln was reported to have replied, "I am not a Freemason, though I have great respect for the institution."

After Lincoln's death, the Grand Master of Masons in the District of Columbia, Benjamin B. French, who had been a friend of Lincoln's, wrote to the editor of the *Masonic Trowel,* who was also the grand secretary of the Grand Lodge of Illinois, "[Lincoln] once told me how highly he respected our Order and that he at one time had fully made up his mind to apply for admission into it." French also wrote to the deputy grand master of the Grand Lodge of New York, in response to a similar inquiry, that Lincoln once told him, in the presence of Mason J. W. Simons, Lincoln had at one time "made up his mind to apply for admission to our Fraternity but feared he was too lazy to attend to his duty as a Mason, as he should like to do, and that he had not carried out his intentions."

The Lincoln biographer Carl Sandburg said, "Though not a Mason, he had at hand a personal copy of the bound *Proceedings of the Grand Royal Arch Chapter of the State of Illinois,* being reports of conventions of the Masonic order for the years 1851–1857."

Succeeding to the presidency when Lincoln was assassinated on April 14, 1865, Andrew Johnson of Tennessee had been a Freemason since 1851. He was probably a member of the Greeneville Chapter No. 82, royal arch Masons. He joined Nashville Commandery of Knights Templar No. 1 in 1859. As president, he received the Scottish Rite degrees in the White House in 1867. Because Radical Republicans in the Senate perceived him as weak and too soft in his policy toward the South, the pretext of Johnson dismissing Secretary of War Edwin M. Stanton, a Mason and Radical sympathizer, from the cabinet was employed to impeach

Johnson. Led by anti-Mason Charles Sumner, freshman congressman and Freemason General Benjamin F. Butler, and former Anti-Mason Party leader Thaddeus Stevens, who had participated in the anti-Mason fervor in the William Morgan affair, the effort failed by one vote in the Senate.

Outside the corridors of government, societies formed to promote white supremacy in the South, including the Men of Justice, the Pale Faces, the Constitutional Union Guards, the White Brotherhood, and the Order of the White Rose. But it was the Ku Klux Klan that would move to the fore. Begun by former Confederate soldiers in Pulaski, Tennessee, in May 1866, the Klan was a disorganized group until 1867. In April of that year at Nashville, Tennessee, General Nathan Bedford Forrest, a heroic cavalry leader of the Confederacy, was chosen "grand wizard of the empire." Each state constituted a "realm" under a "grand dragon," each with a staff of eight "hydras." Several counties formed a "dominion" controlled by a "grand titan." A "province" was ruled by a "grand giant" and four "night hawks." A local "den" was governed by a "grand cyclops" with two night hawks as aides. Members were "ghouls."

A historian of the Klan writes, "Its strange disguises, its silent parades, its midnight rides, its mysterious language and commands, were found to be most effective in playing upon fears and superstitions. The riders muffled their horses' feet and covered the horses with white robes. They themselves, dressed in flowing white sheets, their faces covered with white masks, and with skulls at their saddle horns, posed as spirits of the Confederate dead returned from the battlefields." Although the Klan was often able to achieve its aims by terror alone, lynchings and whippings were used against not only blacks but also so-called carpetbaggers and scalawags.

Concerned about reckless and lawless local leaders, Forrest ordered the disbandment of the Klan and resigned as grand wizard in January 1869. The next year, Congress passed a law to combat the Klan that effectively put it out of business. It remained so until a revival in the years before World War I. Led by William J. Simmons, a former minister and a promoter of fraternal orders, it held its first meeting at Stone Mountain, Georgia. In one form or another, the Klan has existed ever since.

While Freemasonry's connection to the Klan remains a topic of debate, there is no doubt that the revival of Masonry in the second half of the nineteenth century reflected shifts in American customs and attitudes. Historians cite the influence of the Temperance movement to explain Freemasonry taking on aspects of "an 18th-century men's club that carefully separated its ritual meeting from banquets and social functions." Still sensitive to the criticism of clergymen that surfaced during the anti-Masonic period, Freemasonry's teachings moved further from the eighteenth-century Enlightenment philosophy and deism to more closely parallel nineteenth-century religion.

It was a time when other organizations grew directly out of the divisiveness of the Civil War experience. In 1864, the Knights of Pythias was organized by a group of federal clerks in Washington, D.C., who felt that the nation urgently needed to rekindle a brotherly spirit. A ritual designed by Justus H. Rathbone was based on the fourth-century B.C. story of the friendship of Damon and Pythias. A Mason, Rathbone incorporated aspects of Freemasonry. Although the society's motto, "Friendship, Charity, and Benevolence," echoed Freemasonry, the Pythian writer James R. Carnahan said in *Pythian Knighthood,* "We do not, as does Masonry, have clustering about our shrine the clinging ivy of centuries' growth, nor is it yet wreathed about our altars the mysterious legends reaching back into the dim and musty ages of the long ago. We come with present relief for man's present necessities."

After a tour of the post–Civil war South for the U.S. Bureau of Agriculture, Oliver Hudson Kelly (a Freemason) helped found the Order of the Patrons of Husbandry. Called the Grange, it was a fraternal organization to promote agriculture through "cooperation, mutual benefit, and improvement." It was one of the first fraternal organizations to admit women.

The Benevolent and Protective Order of Elks began as a group of actors in New York City. Meeting for lunch and refreshments and at first calling themselves the "Jolly Corks," they organized as a secret, social, and benevolent fraternity with the elk as their symbol and incorporating many Masonic influences.

In 1888, the Loyal Order of Moose was organized in Louisville, Kentucky. Although it did not prosper at first, in 1906 under the direction of John Henry Wilson, a politician and labor activist, the group began to expand. In 1911, it acquired property for a school by purchasing a dairy farm in Illinois to support children who had lost one or both parents. Incorporated as the village of Mooseheart, it became the organization's headquarters.

Founded by Uriah Stevens and other garment workers in Philadelphia in 1869, the Order of Knights of Labor became the first mass organization representing the American working class. A Freemason, Stevens included many features of Masonry in the ritual. The organization added miners in the 1870s and skilled urban tradesmen in the 1880s. The Knights of Labor was one of the few post–Civil War labor organizations that welcomed black members.

Freemasonry historians find a connection between the ideals of Masonry and social groups formed by European immigrants who came to the United States in the late nineteenth and early twentieth centuries. They included the Workmen's Circle (1894), which worked to assimilate Jewish Americans by providing insurance and English lessons, and the Union St. Jean Baptiste, which was formed in 1900 at Woonsocket, Rhode Island, "to unite in a common spirit of brotherhood persons of French origin living in the United States and to promote their collective individual welfare." Of many small societies providing social activities and benefits, the Sons of Italy (1905) became the largest and most influential and soon had 125,000 members nationally.

Organized in 1882, the Knights of Columbus offered Roman Catholic men of varying backgrounds an acceptable fraternal organization. American Catholics found themselves unable to participate in the many fraternal organizations that offered insurance benefits because the church had condemned secret societies. Founded by Michael J. McGivney, a New Haven, Connecticut, parish priest, the Knights of Columbus paralleled the structure of Freemasonry with ritual, degrees, passwords, and the motto "Charity, Unity, Fraternity, and Patriotism."

While the Knights of Columbus enjoyed the approval of the Roman Catholic Church in 1884, the position of Vatican animosity regarding Masonry that was first stated by Pope Clement XII in 1739 had not changed. An encyclical by Leo XIII in 1884 called on each member of the clergy to help defeat Catholicism's old enemy with the words:

> We pray and beseech you, venerable brethren, to join your efforts with Ours, and earnestly to strive for the extirpation of this foul plague, which is creeping through the veins of the body politic.... We wish it to be your rule first of all to tear away the mask from Freemasonry, and to let it be seen as it really is; and by sermons and pastoral letters to instruct the people as to the artifices used by societies of this kind in seducing men and enticing them into their ranks, and as to the depravity of their opinions and the wickedness of their acts.

As the latest papal bull was being read by the Catholic hierarchy in U.S. cities, the number of grand lodges that had been established in states since the end of the Civil War stood at ten (counting the Indian Territory). Comparing the democracy of Freemasonry in the "great land of the West" with English high Masonry's social class "exclusivity," Arthur Edward Waite in *A Encyclopaedia of Freemasonry* writes that the "generous Brotherhood of America" would reap its reward and "Masonry will receive its crown."

Chapter 10

Equality of Moral Men

IN THE EARLY 1800S, FREEMASONRY IN THE UNITED STATES HAD grown rapidly. The Scottish Rite had been brought to America by Stephen Morin in 1761. By 1763, he had organized his own Rite of Perfection of twenty-five degrees in the British West Indies. By 1767, this was taken to North America by an associate, Henry Francken, who established the Lodge of Perfection at Albany, New York. He continued to propagate the rite after Morin's death in 1771 and was succeeded by François Grasse, the Comte de Grasse-Tilly, who had been involved in creation of the Grand Constitutions of 1786 that formed the basis of the "Mother Supreme Council 33°, Ancient and Accepted Scottish Rite," which was formed in 1801 by the Reverend Frederick Dalcho in Charleston, South Carolina.

With the name "Supreme Council of the Thirty-third Degree for the United States of America," it retained jurisdiction over all other states and territories of the United States. For almost seventy years the Scottish Rite in America followed a convoluted course marked by chaos, divisions, rivalries, and schisms. All that changed in 1859 with the election of Albert Pike, who was a poet, lawyer, Civil War general, mystic, and Masonic ritualist as the new Sovereign Grand Commander of the Supreme Council (Southern Jurisdiction).

Born in Boston on December 29, 1809, Pike grew up poor. He was educated in the public schools in Boston. Although he passed examinations for admission to Harvard College, he was unable to attend because of a requirement that two years' tuition be paid in advance or secured by bond. He became a school teacher and taught in country schools in Massachusetts from 1825 to 1831. Venturing west, he joined a trading party from St. Louis to Santa Fe, then to Mexico. On his return, he traveled the "Staked Plains" and Indian Territory and settled at Van Buren, Arkansas, where he opened a school. He studied law and was admitted to the bar in 1834.

At the outbreak of the Mexican War, he joined the army and was in action at Buena Vista. After he returned to Arkansas, he entered Masonry and became a Master Mason in Western Star Lodge No. 1, Little Rock. Fascinated with its symbolism, he felt "as a Puritan would if a Buddhist ceremony were performed in a Calvinistic church." To learn about the Scottish Rite, he went to Charleston, embraced it and received the degrees from fourth to thirty-second in 1843 and the thirty-third in 1857 (at New Orleans). The following year he gave a lecture on the evil consequences of schisms and disputes in Masonry. Elected sovereign grand commander of the Supreme Council Southern Jurisdiction in 1859, he examined the rites and rituals and found "a chaotic mass" of "incoherent nonsense and jargon." So many pains had been taken to conceal the meaning of the symbols, he said, that their true meaning was for the most part lost, and "ignorance or dullness had supplied others, invented by themselves."

Copying all the rituals "so as to have them in uniform and available shape," he produced "a memorandum book of 400 pages." Of this task, he wrote, "After accumulating a good quantity of material, by reading and copying, I commenced on the Scottish Rite. I found it almost equivalent, as to the degrees I selected, to making something out of nothing. I first endeavored to find, in the degree I had under consideration, a leading idea: and then to carry that out and give the degree as high a character as I could."

The study of the Rite left him feeling that its rituals were "for the most part a lot of worthless trash." In a pamphlet in 1887 he said that the rituals of the degrees of the Ancient and Accepted Scottish Rite that he found "were not impressive in any way." He wrote that no man of intellect and knowledge could regard them "with any respect." Trivial, insipid, and without originality, as "literary productions" they were "contemptible" collections "flat, dull, commonplace." Taking the material home to Arkansas, he "copied the whole of them." The result was *Morals and Dogmas of the Ancient and Accepted Scottish Rite of Freemasonry*. It was an attempt to provide a framework for understanding the religions and philosophies of the ancient past. He felt that without understanding the history of a concept, one could not grasp the concept itself. He did not assert that *Morals and Dogmas* contained all the beliefs of Freemasonry, but only information about ancient cultures, religions, beliefs, and customs in a single book.

Suddenly the best-known Freemason in the United States and the most prolific writer and philosopher of the Craft, he lived during a time of colorful personalities. Knowing many of them, and counting most of them among his friends, he became a familiar figure in the nation's capital. An avowed Whig and antisecessionist, he was a prominent lawyer and large landowner in Little Rock, Arkansas, until 1861. Appointed Confederate commissioner to the tribes of Indian Territory, he brought the Creek, Seminole, Chickasaw, Chocktaw, and Cherokee Nations into alliance with the Confederacy. Being commissioned a brigadier general in the confederate army, he commanded a brigade of Indians at the Battle of Pea Ridge. When they refused to pursue Union forces beyond their territories, he was accused of failing to rally and reorganize his troops and resigned his commission in 1862. Like most confederate officers, he was indicted for treason by the United States, but eventually had his civil rights restored. After the war, he resided in Memphis, Tennessee, and edited the *Memphis Appeal* until 1867. The following year he moved to Washington, D.C., and practiced law in the federal courts until 1880. For the rest of his life, he devoted himself to writing legal treatises and promoting the Masonic order. He died on April 2, 1891, while sitting at his desk in the Scottish Rite Temple in Washington. To American Masonry, he was a leader who "found the Scottish Rite in a log cabin and left it in a Temple."

When Pike died, the backlash that resulted in the anti-Mason fever following the scandal of the William Morgan affair was a distant memory. Another consequence of the Morgan episode was the effect it had on the birth and development of Mormonism. The Church of Jesus

Christ of Latter-day Saints, commonly called the Mormons, was founded by Joseph Smith. He was a Master Mason in Ontario Lodge No. 23, Canandaigua, New York. An older son, Hyrum Smith, belonged to Mount Moriah Lodge No. 112, Palmyra, New York. Smith translated the Book of Mormon from gold plates that he said the angel Moroni revealed to him. His new religion drew converts rapidly, but in the wake of the Morgan scandal involving Freemasons, upstate New York was swept into the anti-Masonic fervor. People were eager to believe the worst about anything they didn't understand, especially if it involved a "secret society."

Hundreds of articles and pamphlets appeared with the common assertion that contents of the Mormon scripture had been influenced by Masonry. Given the rise of the Anti-Mason Party, the publicity from stage presentations mocking the Craft, and public claims that Smith had used Masonic work to produce the Book of Mormon, the new sect and Freemasonry became so interwoven in the public mind that they were one and the same. Typical of this jaundiced view was an article with the headline: MORMONISM—RELIGIOUS FANATICISM—CHURCH AND STATE PARTY.

The item read:

> New York has been celebrated for her parties—her sects—her explosions—her curiosities of human character—her fanaticism political and religious. The strangest parties and wildest opinions originate among us. The human mind in our rich vales—on our sunny hills—in our crowded cities or thousand villages—or along the shores of our translucent lakes bursts beyond all ordinary trammels; throws aside with equal fastidiuousness the maxims of age and the discipline of generations, and strikes out new paths for itself. In politics—in religion—in all the great concerns of man, New York has a character peculiarly her own; strikingly original, purely American—energetic and wild to the very farthest boundaries of imagination. The center of the state is quiet comparatively, and grave to a degree; but its two extremities, Eastern and Western; the city of the Atlantic, and the continuous villages of the Lakes, contain all that is curious

in human character—daring in conception—wild in invention, and singular in practical good sense as well as in solemn foolery.

You have heard of MORMONISM—who has not? Paragraph has followed paragraph in the newspapers, recounting the movements, detailing their opinions and surprising distant readers with the traits of a singularly new religious sect which had its origin in this state. Mormonism is the latest device of roguery, ingenuity, ignorance and religious excitement combined, and acting on materials prepared by those who ought to know better. It is one of the mental exhalations of Western New York.

The individuals who gave birth to this species of fanaticism are very simple personages, and not known until this thrust them into notice. The first of these persons, Smith, resided on the borders of Wayne and Ontario counties on the road leading from Canandaigua to Palmyra. Old Joe Smith had been a country pedlar in his younger days, and possessed all the shrewdness, cunning, and small intrigue which are generally and justly attributed to that description of persons. He was a great story teller, full of anecdotes picked up in his peregrinations—and possessed a tongue as smooth as oil and as quick as lightning. He had been quite a speculator in a small way in his younger days, but had been more fortunate in picking up materials for his tongue than stuff for the purse. Of late years he picked up his living somewhere in the town of Manchester by following a branch of the "American System"—the manufacture of gingerbread and such like domestic wares. In this article he was a considerable speculator, having on hand during a fall of price no less than two baskets full, and I believe his son, Joe, Junior, was at times a partner in the concern. What their dividends were I could not learn, but they used considerable molasses, and were against the duty on that article. Young Joe, who afterwards figured so largely in the Mormon religion, was at that period a careless, indolent, idle, and shiftless fellow. He hung around the villages and strolled round the taverns without any end or aim—without any positive defect or as little merit in his character. He was rather a stout able bodied fellow, and might have made a good living in such a country as this where any one who is willing to work, can soon get on in the world. He was however, the son of a speculative Yankee pedlar, and was brought up to live by his wits. Harris also one of the fathers of Mormonism was a substantial farmer near Palmyra—full of passages of the scripture—rather wild and flighty in his talk occasionally—but holding a very respectable character in his neighborhood for sobriety, sense and hard working.

With disdainful and mocking tone, the article continued:

A few years ago the Smiths and others who were influenced by their notions, caught an idea that money was hid in several of the hills which give variety to the country between the Canandaigua Lake and Palmyra on the Erie Canal. Old Smith had in his peddling excursions picked up many stories of men getting rich in New England by digging in certain places and stumbling upon chests of money. The fellow excited the imagination of his few auditors, and made them all anxious to lay hold of the bilk axe and the shovel. As yet no fanatical or religious character had been assumed by the Smiths. They exhibited the simple and ordinary desire of getting rich by some short cut if possible. With this view the Smiths and their associates commenced digging, in the numerous hills which diversify the face of the country in the town of Manchester. The sensible country people paid slight attention to them at first. They knew them to be a thriftless set, more addicted to exerting their wits than their industry, readier at inventing stories and tales than attending church or engaging in any industrious trade. On the sides & in the slopes of several of these hills, these excavations are still to be seen. They would occasionally conceal their purposes, and at other times reveal them by such snatches as might excite curiosity. They dug these holes by day, and at night talked and dreamed over the counties' riches they should enjoy, if they could only hit upon an iron chest full of dollars. In excavating the grounds, they began by taking up the green sod in the form of a circle of six feet diameter—then would continue to dig to the depth of ten, twenty, and sometimes thirty feet. At last some person who joined them spoke of a person in Ohio near Painesville, who had a particular felicity in finding out the spots of ground where money is hid and riches obtained. He related long stories how this person had been along shore in the east—how he had much experience in money digging—how he dreamt of the very spots where it could be found.

The scathing article asserted:

After the lapse of some weeks the expedition was completed, and the famous Ohio man made his appearance among them. This recruit was the most cunning, intelligent, and odd of the whole. He had been a preacher of almost every religion and a teacher of all sorts of morals. He was perfectly au fait with every species of prejudice, folly or fanaticism, which governs the mass of enthusiasts. In the course of his experience, he had attended all sorts of camp-meetings, prayer meetings, anxious meetings, and revival meetings. He knew every turn of the human mind in relation to these matters. He had a superior knowledge of human nature, considerable talent, great plausibility, and knew how to work the passions as exactly as a Cape Cod sailor knows how to work a whale ship. His name I believe is Henry Rangdon or Ringdon, or some such word. About the time that this person appeared among them, a splendid excavation was begun in a long narrow hill, between Manchester and Palmyra. This hill has since been called by some, the Golden Bible Hill.

Because of such vituperation, Smith and his followers fled from New York to Ohio and Illinois. Locals immediately became suspicious of the economic and political power of Mormons and despised their practice of polygamy. The historical record of Freemasonry among the Mormons starts on April 6,1840, when the Grand Lodge of Illinois was formed by Judge and General James Adams, the Mormon patriarch. The Mormon Church had been founded on April 6, 1830, and a "Nauvoo Temple" was dedicated on that day, which Mormons believe is the actual birth date of Jesus Christ. Early years of the Grand Lodge in Illinois were

fraught with difficulty and not all lodges within the state joined it until
the middle of the 1840s.

The Freemason scholar Terry Chateau writes, "Under the Grand
Mastership of a complex and colorful individual, named Abraham Jonas
and a Deputy Grand Master named James Adams, the new Grand Lodge
engaged in some unusual transactions" with the Mormons of Nauvoo.
Motives of those involved in the unusual transactions have puzzled
Masonic scholars throughout the years. Called "one of the most devious
and controversial performances American Freemasonry has ever engaged
in," it involved what Chateau terms "two self-serving opportunistic par-
tisan politicians," Deputy Grand Master James Adams and Grand Master
Abraham Jonas, who induced Joseph Smith to allow the introduction of
Freemasonry in Nauvoo.

Chateau states that they planned on treating it as an elitist group
open only to a select few, but Joseph Smith insisted that it be open to
every holder of the Mormon priesthood who had the interest to petition
for admittance into Masonry. The sole exception would be the peti-
tioner who had exceptionally negative qualities, known and acknowledged as such. Smith insisted that the Nauvoo Lodge be all inclusive. It
had three lodges in Illinois and two in Iowa, collectively known as the
"Mormon lodges." The Nauvoo Lodge had a total membership of 1,550
Masons. A conservative estimate of the membership of the other four
lodges suggests that the total of the five lodges may have exceeded 2,000.
Minutes of the Nauvoo Lodge for March 15, 1842, show that Grand
Master Jonas (Illinois Grand Master) opened the lodge in the third de-
gree of Masonry and conducted a public installation of Nauvoo Lodge
at a grove near the temple. The minutes then go on to show that both
Joseph Smith and Sidney Rigdon were initiated Entered Apprentice
Masons during the day. The record for March 16 lists the two candi-
dates and shows that they were made Fellowcraft and Master Masons.
The first five presidents of the Mormon Church—Joseph Smith, Brigham
Young, John Taylor, Wilford Woodruff, and Lorenzo Snow—were all
made Masons in Nauvoo Lodge.

After Freemasonry was introduced to Nauvoo, the lodge meetings
were in the upper room of Smith's general store while the new Masonic

hall was being built. This was dedicated by Hyrum Smith on April 5, 1844, and was used by the church and community for many activities. The church restored the building and called it the "Cultural Hall–Masonic Hall." The weather vane placed on the temple depicted an angel in priestly robes with the Book of Mormon in one hand and a trumpet in the other. The angel has a cap on his head and above him are the Masonic square and compass. Religious antagonism and physical conflict increased and finally came to a head with the violent deaths of Joseph and Hyrum Smith.

Joseph was a Mason in good standing of Nauvoo Lodge, while Hyrum was the incumbent master of the lodge. On the morning of June 27, 1844, the citizens of Warsaw, Illinois, held a meeting and adopted a resolution to go to Nauvoo and exterminate the city and its Mormons. Colonel Levi Williams called together his regiment of militia and marched to Carthage, where the Smiths had surrendered themselves following a pledge of safety by the governor. Williams and his men were met on the road with an order from the governor that disbanded the regiment. About 150 of Williams's men blacked their faces with mud and gunpowder. Arrangements were made for the guards at the jail to charge their guns with blanks, which they would fire at the disguised militiamen when they attacked the jail. This plan was carried out and the Smiths and a pair of the visitors, John Taylor and Willard Richards, threw themselves against the door to prevent the mob from entering. Shot were fired through the door, killing Hyrum instantly. Joseph Smith fired a pistol that had been smuggled to him and wounded four men. Having exhausted his ammunition, and with the mob still trying to break down the door, he attempted to escape by jumping out a window, but was stunned by the two-story fall. When he hit the ground, someone picked him up. Smith recognized Masons in the mob and cried out "Oh Lord, My God." His words were cut of by a volley of musket balls.

Smith's successor was Brigham Young. Born on June 1, 1801, at Whitingham, Vermont, the ninth of eleven children, he was raised in a frontier settlement and had only eleven days of formal schooling. He worked as a carpenter, joiner, painter, and glazier. According to William R. Denslow in *10,000 Famous Freemasons*, he belonged to Milnor Lodge

No. 303, Victor, New York, but in lodge membership lists sent to New York Grand Lodge until 1830 his name does not appear. Another account says that he entered into the Craft at the Nauvoo Lodge on April 9, 1842.

From Illinois, Young led between 60,000 and 70,000 pioneers to the Salt Lake Valley in Utah, arriving on July 24, 1847. They established the center of the Church of Jesus Christ of Latter-day Saints. Named president and prophet of the church, he became the first governor of the Territory of Utah and was successful in securing economic and political rights for Mormons. He was the first superintendent of Indian Affairs of Utah Territory and church president for thirty years. A Mormon history states that Young "was both a seeker for personal religious contentment and a pragmatist looking for what he understood to be the primitive church of the New Testament," but that after first confronting the Book of Mormon as a young married man, he was not an immediate convert. He is quoted as saying "I examined the matter studiously for two years before I made up my mind to receive the book. I knew it was true, as well as I knew I could see with my own eyes, or feel with the touch of my fingers. Had not this been the case, I never would have embraced it to this day, I wished time sufficient to prove all things for myself."

Before leading the Mormon pioneers west, he'd been a Mormon missionary in Canada and throughout the eastern United States and Great Britain. During a twenty-two-month stay he brought between 7,000 and 8,000 new members into the faith. When he returned to Utah, he wrote in his diary, "This evening I am with my love alone by the fireside for the first time in years." He died on August 29, 1877, in Salt Lake City at the age of seventy-six. His statue stands in the rotunda of the Capitol of Washington, D.C. Of his accomplishments he said, "I care nothing about my character in this world. I do not care what men say about me. I want my character to stand fair in the eyes of my Heavenly Father."

When the first Mormon pioneer company entered the Salt Lake Valley under Young's leadership, a significant body of Masons entered with him. As of that date, the full Mormon hierarchy was comprised of Masons. A review of the 143 men who entered the valley shows how prevalent Masonry had become among the Mormons. Three of the group were black slaves, 16 were young men not yet of age, leaving 124 who might possibly have been of the Craft. Of these, there were ten whose age was not known. The others were not known to be Masons.

A Mormon biography of Young states, "Knowing both Mormonism and Freemasonry in depth, Brigham Young realized that nothing constructive or positive could result from a series of continuing exchanges over the years. He instituted an inflexible policy that the Mormon Church would have nothing to say publicly regarding Freemasonry."

This position was steadfastly and discretely adhered to for almost a century and a half, with few exceptions. Yet, there is evidence that Young took his Masonry seriously and afforded studious attention to its meaning and significance. Numerous photographs and paintings show him wearing Masonic pins.

A Mormon historian records, "A vast majority of Mormon Masons took their Masonic obligations seriously and deeply to heart. Great numbers were devoted and dedicated Masons who truly loved the Order. Freemasonry among Mormons was not merely a fraternity. Lodge meetings were serious convocations entirely devoid of the jovial lightheartedness and the strenuous, physical horseplay which characterized most frontier lodges. Their time and attention were fully occupied with the heavy demands of working the three degrees."

Rituals and symbolism of the Mormon Church, as Freemasonry, symbolize the rituals of King Solomon's Temple. Because the beehive is an emblem of industry and recommends the practice of that virtue, Joseph Smith adopted the beehive as the church and community symbol. Brigham Young added it to his personal seal. He built a large home topped by a gilded beehive. Several of the temples display the beehive prominently on both their interiors and exteriors. It is the sole heraldic device on the shield of the state seal and flag and the seals of the University of Utah and Brigham Young University. An immense beehive was atop the old Hotel Utah. On the Mormon Temple are inscribed several Masonic symbols, including a beehive, the sun, moon, and stars, the "all-seeing-eye," and clasped hands.

The position of American Freemasonry is that "as the oldest fraternity in the world, its ceremonies and forms have been copied, either consciously or unconsciously, throughout the past three centuries, as in the many fraternal societies that flourished in the late 1800s. Freemasonry also notes that its forms and ceremonies did not arrive 'fully-formed' and have elements taken from institutions, beliefs, and societies well before Freemasonry's existence."

Visiting Brigham Young in 1861, Mark Twain wrote:

> He was very simply dressed and was just taking off a straw hat as we entered. He talked about Utah, and the Indians, and Nevada, and general American matters and questions, with our secretary and certain government officials who came with us. But he never paid any attention to me, notwithstanding [that] I made several attempts to "draw him out" on federal politics and his high handed attitude toward Congress.... But he merely looked around at me, at distant intervals, something as I have seen a benignant old cat look around to see which kitten was meddling with her tail. By and by, I subsided into an indignant silence, and so sat until the end, hot and flushed, and execrating him in my heart for an ignorant savage.

While Mormonism was dominating the state of Utah, the rest of the United States was in a time of opulence that Twain named the "Gilded Age." During this period of extravagant and optimistic American brashness and confidence, no one embodied the politics and free-wheeling (some say free-booting) era of industrial and banking tycoons better than William McKinley, the Republican president of the United States, and Theodore Roosevelt, the vigorous and unabashedly patriotic vice president.

McKinley had enlisted in an Ohio Infantry unit as a private at the beginning of the Civil War and saw his first action at Carnifex Ferry on September 10, 1861. The following year he had what was probably his most trying and successful military service. He fought in the Battle of South Mountain on September 14, 1862. Three days later, he performed outstanding service at Antietam, the bloodiest of all Civil War battles, on September 17, 1862. For his performance there, he was commissioned a second lieutenant. He was in subsequent battles, including Lexington,

Kernstown, Opequan Creek (Winchester, Virginia), Fisher's and Cedar Creek, all in 1864. During that time, he rose to the rank of captain, and on March 13, 1865, he was brevetted major for gallantry in battle by President Abraham Lincoln.

While managing and overseeing protection of an army hospital, he was made a Mason at Winchester, Virginia. Impressed by the Masonic interactions between Confederate prisoners and Union doctors during a time of war, he strove to find an explanation. After learning the reasons, he presented a petition to Hiram Lodge No. 21, Winchester. As a Union army major, he was made a Mason in a Confederate lodge, receiving all three degrees in three days, May 1, 2, 3, 1865, along side J.B.T. Reed, a Confederate chaplain. When mustered out of service on July 26, 1865, he was acting assistant adjutant general under General S. C. Carroll, who commanded the veteran reserve corps at Washington, D.C.

Resuming civilian life, he went to law school at Albany, New York, and, after admission to the Ohio bar and a few years of law practice, he became a U.S. congressman from Ohio and spent the rest of his life in public office, including service as chairman of the House Ways and Means Committee and governor of Ohio.

In an essay on McKinley's life and Freemasonry, Julian E. Endsley, a thirty-second-degree Mason of San Luis Obispo, California, writes that his Masonic record was "impressive" and he "never forgot Masonry."

In an address at Mount Vernon, Virginia, on December 14, 1899, in a Masonic ceremony marking the centennial of George Washington's death, McKinley said, "The Fraternity justly claims the immortal patriot as one of its members, and the whole human family acknowledges him as one of the greatest benefactors."

McKinley regularly visited lodges in his national travels and in Washington. When a delegation from Columbia Lodge No. 2397 visited him in the White House, it presented to him a certificate of membership in that lodge in London, England. On May 22, 1901, he attended a reception in his honor at California Commandery No. 1, San Francisco. During an imperial council meeting in Washington, he received the Shriners at the White House. Also at the White House he held a reception for the Scottish Rite's Supreme Council (Southern Jurisdiction) on October 23, 1899.

"Those activities," notes Endsley, "typified his regular promotion of and participation in our honorable institution."

A favorite McKinley Masonic story recalls that when General Horatio King asked how McKinley happened to become a Mason, McKinley explained:

> After the [Civil War] battle of Opequam, I went with our surgeon of our Ohio regiment to the field where there were about 5,000 Confederate prisoners under guard. Almost as soon as we passed the guard, I noticed the doctor shook hands with a number of Confederate prisoners. He also took from his pockets a roll of bills and distributed all he had among them. Boy-like, I looked on in wonderment. I didn't know what it all meant. On the way back from camp I asked him, "Did you know these men or ever seen them before?"
>
> "No," replied the doctor, "I never saw them before."
>
> McKinley said, "You gave them a lot of money, all you had about you. Do you ever expect to get it back?"
>
> "Well," said the doctor, "if they are able to pay me back, they will. But it makes no difference to me; they are Brother Masons in trouble and I am only doing my duty."
>
> McKinley said to himself, "If that is Freemasonry I will take some of it for myself."

In 1900, McKinley was reelected president with Theodore Roosevelt as vice president. When McKinley was shot in Buffalo, New York, on September 6, 1901, and died eight days later, Roosevelt became the ninth Mason to serve as president. When he ran for election to the office in his own right in 1904 and promised every American a "square deal," Freemasons did not fail to note that the square was not only an architectural draftsman's tool but also the age-old emblem of the Ancient and Honorable Fraternity of Free and Accepted Masons.

Chapter 11

From Brother Washington to Grand Master Harry

THEODORE ROOSEVELT, THE TWENTY-SIXTH PRESIDENT AND ninth Freemason to be president, bestowed two names on the office and residence of every chief executive, except George Washington. Roosevelt memorably defined the power of presidential persuasion as a "bully pulpit." Furthermore, he extensively renovated the White House by modernizing its electrical wiring and moving the presidential offices from the second floor into an addition that became known as the West Wing. "The changes in the White House," he declared, "have transformed it from a shabby likeness to the ground floor of the Astor House [Hotel] into a simple and dignified dwelling for the head of a great republic."

To find an architect to design the building that the Founding Fathers envisioned as "the President's House" in a gleaming federal capital city, the commissioners of the new "District of Columbia" on the Potomac River announced in 1790 a competition and prize of $500. Hundreds of hopefuls, including Thomas Jefferson (anonymously), submitted blueprints. The winner was James Hoban a young Irish immigrant.

Hoban was born in County Kilkenny, Ireland, in 1758. A Roman Catholic, he ignored centuries of papal edicts against Freemasonry that promised excommunication to any Catholic who joined. It's probable that his father, Edward, belonged to the High Knights Templar of Ireland, Kilwinning Lodge No. 75, but no proof exists. James studied architecture in Dublin and immigrated to America in 1783, the same year that saw the formal end of the Revolutionary War with a peace treaty recognizing the new republic.

Settling in Philadelphia, which was the bustling and growing capital of the United States, he sought work by advertising in the *Pennsylvania Evening Herald* to no avail. At the suggestion of some friends, he moved to Charleston, South Carolina, in 1787 and flourished. He designed a theater, an orphan asylum, and a plantation house on Edisto Island, about twenty miles south of Charleston. When he was invited to enter the contest to design the president's house, he found inspiration in a house in Dublin that was steeped in Masonic fact and legend.

Called the Leinster House, it was a three-story late-Georgian mansion that had been built for the twentieth Earl of Kildare, James Fitzgerald, later made Viscount Leinster by George II and Duke of Leinster by George III ("the king who lost the American colonies"). Leinster was a key figure in Irish Freemasonry. One of his ancestors, Maurice Fitzgerald, invited the Knights Templar to organize banking in Dublin in 1204. On April 26, 1779, James Fitzgerald and Dr. George A. Cunningham appealed to the Master of the Mother Lodge at Kilwinning for permission to form "a lodge of the same name in Dublin." It became Kilwinning Lodge No. 75, also known as the High Knights Templar of Ireland, to which the Hobans, father and son, belonged.

The place chosen for the site of the President's House that Hoban was named to design was a bleak area of scrubland called "the Barrens," but it had a panoramic view of the Potomac River. The White House historian William Seale writes that "broad flats of water were everywhere, silvery, reflecting the sky through dead grass and still wintry-fields." Stonemasons were hired from the local Masonic lodge and imported from Scotland's Lodge No. 8. The cornerstone was laid in a traditional Masonic ceremony on Saturday, October 13, 1792. This date has great significance in Freemasonry, not only because of the number 13 but also because the execution of the Templars in Paris by King Philip occurred on a Friday the thirteenth, hence the stigma of bad luck that persists to any Friday that falls on the thirteenth.

In *The President's House: A History,* Seale describes the cornerstone-laying participants gathering at Georgetown's Fountain Inn as an "orderly formation" and walking the dusty road to the site. "At the head of the parade were the Freemasons, in proper Masonic order by rank; next were the commissioners of the federal district; next the 'Gentlemen of the town and neighborhood'; and last 'The different artificers, et cetera.'"

Mortar was laid atop the foundation stone. Into this was pressed a polished brass plate with the engraving:

> The first stone of the President's House was laid the 13th day of October, and in the seventeenth year of the independence of the United States of America.
>
> George Washington, *President*
> Thomas Johnson, Doctor Stewart, Daniel Carroll, *Commissioners*
> James Hoban, *Architect*
> Collen Williamson, *Master Mason*

After the cornerstone was set atop the plate and tapped into place by Williamson, the men returned to the Fountain Inn for an "elegant dinner," with sixteen toasts, including one to President George Washington. Busy with the affairs of state in Philadelphia, he'd been unable to join his Masonic brethren.

Thirteen months after the ceremony, Hoban and two other Freemasons petitioned the York Rite for a warrant to establish Federal Lodge No. 15. Hoban became its first Master. His illicit Freemasonry did not prevent him from working for the Catholic Church. He is credited with establishing the capital city's first Catholic church, St. Patrick's (1792), and serving on the committee to erect St. Peter's Church on Capitol Hill in 1820. Elected to the Washington City Council in 1802, he served on it intermittently for many years, but in 1814 he found himself again at work on the President's House, this time to reconstruct it from a burned ruin.

Sweeping into the city from Maryland in the summer of 1814, a British army under General Robert Ross put torches to all the government buildings, forcing President James Madison and his wife, Dolly, to flee. Midway through the blaze, a thunderstorm's torrential rain doused the conflagration, leaving the walls of Hoban's building standing, but terribly damaged and blackened. Whitewash was lavishly applied to prevent further deterioration of weakened stonework. Seale notes, "Considering that it had taken nearly ten years to build the first White House, the reconstruction moved along very quickly. The house was finished in slightly less than three years."

The placement of the President's House had been the choice of the architect who'd laid out the plan for the capital city that would be named for the hero acclaimed as "the father of his country," even though George Washington never presided there. A National Park Service history notes that on January 24, 1791, President Washington announced a congressionally designated permanent location of the national capital. It was to be a diamond-shaped ten-mile tract at the confluence of the Potomac and Eastern Branch rivers. After a survey of the area was undertaken by Andrew Ellicott and Benjamin Banneker, forty boundary stones, laid at one-mile intervals, established the boundaries based on celestial calculations by Banneker. A self-taught astronomer of African descent, he was one of the few free blacks living in the vicinity. Within this 100-square-mile diamond called the District of Columbia, a smaller area was laid out as the city of Washington. In 1846, a third of the district was returned by congressional action to Virginia, removing that portion of the original district west of the Potomac River. In March 1791, Major Pierre Charles L'Enfant was chosen to prepare the plan.

Born in France on August 2, 1754, he arrived in America in 1777 and volunteered to join the Revolution. He became a friend of Washington. In 1783, he attained the rank of major. He is not known to have been a Freemason, but he may have been. When Congress decided to build the capital city on the Potomac, he asked Washington to allow him to prepare a design. Even though Washington dismissed him the following year because of L'Enfant's insistence on complete control of the project, the plan was retained. It was inspired by André Lenôtre's plan for the palace and garden of Versailles, where L'Enfant's father had worked as a court painter. It also borrowed from Domenico Fontana's 1585 scheme for the replanning of Rome under Pope Sixtus V. The avenues were to be "wide, grand, lined with trees, and situated in a manner that would visually connect ideal topographical site throughout the city, where important structures, monuments, and fountains were to be erected."

On paper, L'Enfant shaded and numbered fifteen large open spaces at the intersections of these avenues and indicated that they would be divided among the states. He specified that each reservation would feature statues and memorials to honor worthy citizens. The open spaces were as integral to the capital as the buildings to be erected around them. It was L'Enfant's opposition to selling land prematurely and refusal to furnish his map to the city commissioners in time for the sale that resulted in Washington's reluctant decision to relieve him of his duties. Andrew Ellicott, a surveyor, reproduced L'Enfant's plan from memory.

"In the context of the United States," notes the National Park Service history, "a plan as grand as the 200 year old city of Washington, DC, stands alone in its magnificence and scale. But as the capital of a new nation, its position and appearance had to surpass social, economic and cultural balance of a mere city. It was intended as the model for American city planning and a symbol of governmental power to be seen by other nations."

Although L'Enfant died penniless and alone in 1825, he was reinterred to Arlington National Cemetery. If he could return to his city today, he would find that his design has been interpreted as an expression of Freemasonry conspiracy with Satanic underpinnings, that there was a Masonic purpose in the layout of Washington and its buildings that was part of an ongoing conspiracy to place the United States at the center of a "New World Order." The basis of this is assertions by individuals and groups that the city plan consists of the Masonic symbols of the square, the rule, the pentagram, and the compass. They contend that the Capitol Building is the top of a compass, the left leg is Pennsylvania Avenue, and the right leg is Maryland Avenue. The left leg stands on the Jefferson Memorial. The right rests on the White House. This design also forms the head and ears of a Satanic goat's head.

An inverted five-pointed star called a pentagram (a Masonic symbol) sits on top of the White House and is formed within the intersections of

Connecticut and Vermont avenues northward to Dupont and Logan circles, with Massachusetts Avenue extending to Washington Circle to the west and Mount Vernon Square on the east. "The center of the pentagram," says an Internet Web site on the subject, "is 16th Street, where thirteen blocks due north of the very center of the White House, the Masonic House of the Temple sits at the top of this occult iceberg."

Furthermore, the Washington Monument, with all its supposed Masonic symbolism, is in "perfect line to the intersecting point of the form of the Masonic square." Cornerstones of all these building and others have been laid out in Masonic ritual and dedicated to the "demonic god of Masonry." This deity is "JaoBulOn," a secret name or the "Lost Word" that is "learned in the ritual of the Royal Arch Degree." The name consists of *Jao* (Greek for "Jehovah"), *Bul* (rendering of the biblical pagan god Baal), and *On* (the Babylonian Christ-like Osiris).

Beyond the geography of Washington, D.C., those who interpret sinister occult meaning and Masonic influences in the structure of the U.S. government point to the Great Seal of the United States. Its creation began late in the afternoon of July 4, 1776. The Continental Congress resolved that "Dr. Franklin, Mr. Adams and Mr. Jefferson be a committee to prepare a device for a Seal of the United States of America." On August 20, the committee reported its design to Congress; but the report was tabled. For three and a half years, no further action was taken. On March 25, 1780, the report of the first committee was referred to a new committee consisting of James Lovell, John Morin Scott, and William Churchill Houston. This committee received artistic assistance from Francis Hopkinson. A new design was reported on May 10 (or 11), 1780. Debate was followed by recommittal to the committee with no further progress for two more years. In the spring of 1782, a third committee, consisting of Arthur Middleton, John Rutledge, and Elias Boudinot with the assistance of William Barton, reported a third design for a seal to Congress that was found not satisfactory. On June 13, 1782, Congress referred all the committee reports to Charles Thomason, the secretary of Congress. Thomason wrote his report to Congress and submitted it on June 20, 1782. The report was accepted the same day.

Adherents of the belief in Masonic meanings in the design of Washington, D.C., find them in the Great Seal. According to them, of those who helped to design it, "the following are known to have been Masons: Benjamin Franklin, Thomas Jefferson, William Churchhill Houston, and William Barton." It is impossible to assert whether they drew heavily on Freemasonry in this work, continues the theory, but when an "informed" Freemason examines the great seal, he sees:

> On the obverse is an eagle whose dexter wing has thirty-two feathers, the number of ordinary degrees in Scottish Rite Freemasonry. The sinister wing has thirty-three feathers, the additional feather corresponding to the Thirty-third Degree of the same Rite conferred for outstanding Masonic service. The tail feathers number nine, the number of degrees in the Chapter, Council, and Commandery of the York Rite of Freemasonry. Scottish Rite Masonry had its origin in France; the York Rite is sometimes called the American Rite; the eagle thus clothed represents the union of French and American Masons in the struggle for Liberty, Equality, and Fraternity.

The total number of feathers in the two wings is sixty-five, which is the value of the Hebrew phrase *yam yawchod* (together in unity). This phrase appears in Psalm 133: "Behold, how good and how pleasant it is for brethren to dwell together in unity." The verse is used in the ritual of the first degree of Freemasonry. The glory above the eagle's head in the seal is divided into twenty-four equal parts, reminding the observer of the Mason's gauge, which is also divided into twenty-four equal parts and is emblematic of the service a Mason is obligated to perform.

The five-pointed star represents the Masonic Blazing Star and the five points of fellowship. An arrangement of the stars in a constellation forms overlapping equilateral triangles and the Star of David, which calls to mind King David's dream of building a temple, the "Companions" who rebuilt a desecrated temple, and the finding of "the Word that was lost." The gold, silver, and azure colors represent the sun, moon, and worshipful master. The first rules the day, the second the night, and the third the lodge.

The shield on the eagle's breast affirms by its colors: valor (red), purity (white), and justice (blue), which are the Masonic cardinal virtues. The scroll in the eagle's beak, bearing the words *E Pluribus Unum* (of the many), means the unity that has made "brothers of many." The all-seeing eye within a triangle surrounded by a golden glory represents the capstone of the unfinished pyramid and conveys the immortality of the soul and that in eternity a Mason will complete the capstone of his earthly labors according to the designs of the Supreme Architect of the Universe. The unfinished pyramid reminds a Mason of the unfinished Temple and the death of its master architect, Hiram Abiff. The blaze of glory found on either side of the great seal reminds the Mason of the "Great Light in Masonry," which is the rule and guide to faith and practice and without which no Masonic lodge can exist.

These points of significance, say Masons with a sardonic tone:

> Lead to the conclusion that investigators in the fields of history and government have overlooked an influence in forming the government of the United States that may well have been as important as economic pressures of the age. It also appears that the political theorists have overlooked an important influence in the evolution of American democracy that may be defined as broader than a special political form, a method of conducting government by means of officials elected by popular suffrage; a democracy in which these processes are only a means, the best means for realizing the idealistic goals for the full development of human potentialities. This democracy is a way of life, social and individual, founded on faith in the human capacity and intelligence and in the just power of accumulated and cooperative experience; and in equality before the law and in its administration and in the right to have and express opinion—a democracy whose final definition coincides with that of Freemasonry.

The design was accepted on May 9, 1782, and referred to Charles Thompson (a Mason), the secretary of Congress, on June 13. The final version, which was approved and adopted by an act of Congress on June 20, 1782, was the result of a series of committee meetings that combined ideas from Barton, Thompson, and Jefferson, who placed a triangle around the eye, added "1776," "E Pluribus Unum," the olive branch on the front, the stars above the eagle, and a few other things. Within weeks, a brass plate of the face of the Great Seal was produced, but not of the reverse side. Although the design of the seal was not to deviate from the one approved, when the original wore out, and a second engraving in 1841 was ordered by Secretary of State Daniel Webster, the design by the French artist R. P. Lamplier and cut by John V. N. Throop had subtle differences, such as six, rather than thirteen arrows, and the phoenix clearly became an eagle. Referred to as the Websterian Great Seal, it was used until 1885. A third engraving was prepared in that year under Secretary of State F. T. Frelinghuysen and cut by Tiffany and Company. A fourth under Secretary of State John Hay was engraved by Max Zeiler and cut by Baily, Banks and Biddle; both were consistent with the design passed by law in 1782.

A committee appointed by Frelinghuysen, consisting of Theodore F. Dwight (chief of the Bureau of Rolls and Library of the State Department), Justin Winsor (historian), Charles Eliot Norton (Harvard professor), William H. Whitmore (genealogist), John Denison Chaplin Jr. (associate editor of *American Cyclopedia*), and James Horton Whitehouse (designer for Tiffany and Company in New York City) decided that a die for the reverse side of the seal would not be produced and used as an official seal. Norton called it a "dull emblem of a Masonic fraternity." *The Seal of the United States,* a 1957 pamphlet by the U.S. Government Printing Office, indicated that in 1885 "a die may have been cut," but never used.

In 1917, Celestia Root Lang (editor and publisher of *Divine Life* magazine from the Independent Theosophical Society of America) wrote, "The reverse side must have been designed by a mystic, one versed in symbolism."

In *The Coming of the New Deal,* Arthur M. Schlesinger Jr. states that Vice President Henry A. Wallace (a Mason) was "fascinated" by the occult. He was impressed enough with the significance of the reverse side of the great seal to lobby Treasury Secretary Henry Morgenthau Jr. to have it put on the back of the one-dollar bill in 1935.

What this gesture meant, according to those who find symbols of Masonic conspiracy, is that Masons had finally reached the point where they could set into motion their plans for the New World Order. The mystical number 13 is proof of this. The Great Seal has thirteen stars in the crest, thirteen stripes and bars in the shield, thirteen olives, thirteen arrows in the right claw, thirteen feathers in the arrows, thirteen letters in "Annuit Coeptis," thirteen letters in "E Pluribus Unum," thirteen courses of stone in the pyramid and 27 dots in the divisions around the crest. There are also thirty-two feathers on the right wing of the eagle, representing the thirty-two degrees in Scottish Rite Masonry, and there are thirty-three feathers on the left, which represent thirty-three degrees of the York Rite Freemasonry. The pyramid has thirteen levels. Within the capstone is an eye, but is not the eye of God. It stems from Masonic tradition, where it is known as the Eye of Horus (the sun god), or all-seeing eye, referring to the protection of Providence, "whose eye never slumbers nor sleeps," and alluding to the "Big Brother" system of constant surveillance.

The pyramid supposedly represents the organizational structure of the New World Order, and the capstone containing the eye represents the House of Rothschild, a banking family who controls the group and has perpetuated the goal of a one-world government.

The Treasury Department issued a press release on August 15, 1935, that gave details of the symbol on the back of the one-dollar bill: "The eye and triangular glory symbolize an all-seeing Deity. The pyramid is the symbol of strength and its unfinished condition denoted the belief of the designers of the Great Seal that there was still work to be done."

Conspiracy theorists note the press release says "Deity," not "God."

The news release also indicated that the Latin phrase *Annuit Coeptis* translates as "he (God) favored our undertakings," and came from Virgil's *audacibus annue coeptis,* or "favor my daring undertaking." This phrase refers to the "golden age" during which the "Saturnian" (Saturn was the father of Osiris) kingdom shall return. *Novus Ordo Seclorum* translates as "a new order of the ages," from Virgil's *magnus ab integro seclorum nascitur ordo,* or "the great series of ages begins anew." The combination of the two Latin phrases means "Announcing the Birth of a New Secular Order." The date 1776 at the base of the pyramid in Roman numerals does not refer to July 4, but to May 1, "May Day," an international holiday for all workers which was established in 1889 at the International Socialist Congress.

Whether these interpretations of the Great Seal and its place on the dollar were signs of a vast secret plot for world domination were true did not appear to concern President Warren G. Harding. He was not a socialist, nor was he seeking to take over the world. Even if he'd wanted to, he died in office in 1923.

Harry S Truman, arguably the most accomplished in Freemasonry of the presidents, had the distinction of claiming significance in being Masonry's thirteenth. He was also famous for having a placard on his desk that said "The buck stops here." He entered the Craft on December 21, 1908, in Belton Lodge No. 450, Grandview, Missouri. He recalled in his memoirs that he had seen a man on a street wearing a Masonic pin and told him he'd always wanted to be a Mason. A few days later, the man gave him an application. He received the degree of Entered Apprentice on February 9, 1909. The following year he accepted the station of Junior Warden. In 1911, several members of Belton Lodge separated to establish Grandview Lodge No. 618. Truman was made its first Worshipful Master. Later, he served as secretary of the lodge, and in 1917, when leaving to serve as an artillery captain in World War I, he was again Master of the Lodge. After the war, he was district deputy grand lecturer and district deputy grand master of the Fifty-ninth Masonic District. He remained in these stations from 1925 until his appointment in the Grand Lodge line in 1930. In September 1940, when the Grand Lodge met, he was running for the U.S. Senate. He was elected Grand Master and a few weeks later was elected senator. During his year as Grand Master, Congress was in session most of the time, but he found time to make individual visits to nineteen Missouri Masonic lodges, six district associations, and a few conferences of district deputies. He presented several fifty-year pins, visited the Grand Lodges of Texas and the District of Colombia, and attended an anniversary gathering of Philadelphia Lodge. He represented Missouri at a Washington conference of grand masters in February 1941, where he presented Missouri's check for $1,900 to a Washington memorial at Alexandria.

As president of the United States, he enlisted the Library of Congress to furnish the Masonic Research Lodge of Missouri with copies of reference cards on Freemasonry. He again aided the Missouri Lodge of Research by writing the forward for the first volume of William R. Denslow's *10,000 Famous Freemasons* (1957). During his presidency, he initiated more than thirty candidates with the "strict injunction" that no publicity was to come from his participation. His received degrees in Orient Chapter No. 102, Kansas City, on November 11 and 15, 1919, and Shekinah Council No. 24, Kansas City, on December 18, 1919; and the orders of knighthood in Palestine Commandery No. 17, Independence, on June 7 and 15, 1923. His Scottish Rite degrees were received in Kansas City, January 24, March 27, 30, and 31, 1917. On October 19, 1945, he received the Thirty-third degree at Washington, D.C., while president. He became a member of Ararat Shrine Temple, Kansas City, April 2, 1917, and was the orator of that body in 1932, marshal in 1933, and second ceremonial master in 1934. He became a member of the Royal Order of Jesters, Kansas City, Court No. 54, on December 18, 1931. He was also a member of Mary Conclave, Red Cross of Constantine, Kansas City. He was the grand representative of the Grand Lodge of Scotland near the Grand Lodge of Missouri.

When Truman ordered a renovation and rebuilding of the White House, he hoped the workers would find the Masonic commemorative plate that was placed on the foundation stone. With the interior walls exposed, Seale writes, Truman "quickly began to notice the marks of identification left by the original stonemasons." Seale's account continues:

> He pronounced the marks "Masonic"—which was in part correct, as it turned out—and ordered all he could see extracted, some to be set into the walls of the restored ground floor kitchen and the rest sent to the grand lodges of the Masonic orders of every state in the Union, along with a letter which read in part: "I place in your hands a stone taken from the walls of the White House... These evidences

of the number of members of the Craft who built the President's off-
ical residence so intimately aligns Freemasonry with the formation
and founding of our Government that I believe your Grand Lodge
will cherish this link between the Fraternity and the Government of
the Nation, of which the White House is the symbol."

In the oral biography *Plain Speaking*, the author Merle Miller asked
Truman about public fears of Freemasonry's secretiveness. Truman
replied, "I've got every degree on the Masons that there is, and if there
are any secrets to give away, I'll be damned if I know what they are."

Chapter 12

The Business of America

WHEN HARRY S TRUMAN WAS BORN IN 1884, THERE WERE more than 300 Masonic orders with a total fraternal membership exceeding 6 million. One observer noted that businessmen and politicians used the orders to cultivate contacts and establish ties with clients and like-minded people elsewhere. Others found satisfaction in exotic rituals that provided a religious experience that was free of "liberal Protestantism" and a masculine "family" vastly different from the one in which most members had been raised. Some reasoned that if George Washington, Andrew Jackson, William McKinley, and Theodore Roosevelt were Masons, it must be a worthwhile bunch. Even Roosevelt's successor in the White House belonged.

William Howard Taft had been made a Mason "on sight" when he was president-elect by Charles C. Hoskinson, the Grand Master of Ohio, on February 18, 1900. Because being immediately admitted to the Craft meant that Taft did not have to go through rituals that included being half naked, blindfolded with a hood (the origin of the word *hoodwink*), and led around with a rope around the neck, the brothers of the lodge were spared looking at Taft's 300-plus-pound body. The instant initiation provoked Walter Hurt, a Taft enemy and publisher of an anti-Catholic periodical, to publish the article "Taft: A 35-Minute Mason." American Freemasons thought that Taft represented the Craft "well enough" and appreciated his participation in public ceremonies, including wearing a Masonic apron depicting George Washington holding a trowel during the laying of the cornerstone of the Capitol.

During World War I, thousands of American Masons who went "over there" found fraternal welcome from their English and French brethren. They came home to a postwar America in which Republican presidential candidate and Masonic brother Warren G. Harding of Ohio promised in 1920 to return the United States to "normalcy." War-weary voters responded enthusiastically and made him their twenty-ninth chief executive and Freemasonry's eleventh.

Harding was born near Marion, Ohio, on November 2, 1865. An active civic leader, he became the publisher of a newspaper, a trustee of the Trinity Baptist Church, a director of almost every important business, and a leader in fraternal organizations and charitable enterprises. He was initiated in Freemasonry on June 28, 1901, in Marion Lodge No. 70, Marion, Ohio, but antagonism in the lodge hindered his advancement until 1920, by which time he had been nominated for president. Friends persuaded the opposition to withdraw the objection. Nineteen years after his initiation, he achieved the Sublime Degree of Master Mason in Marion Lodge. In 1920, he was elected with an unprecedented landslide of 60 percent of the popular vote.

When he took office, a young English Freemason named Manly P. Hall published a book with the provocative title *The Lost Keys of Freemasonry* (also known as *The Secret of Hiram Abiff*). It proved to be the most sensational publication on the subject of Freemasonry since the ill-fated 1827 posthumous exposé by William Morgan. Born in Peterborough, Ontario, on March 18, 1901, Hall was raised by a grandmother who brought him to the United States. From an early age, he studied the broad range of the world's ancient wisdom traditions. "Unlike so many of his contemporaries," notes a biographer, "he concluded that wisdom was not to be found on only one path or in only one religion. Instead, he saw wisdom as the highest realm where philosophy, religion, and science come together without boundaries."

Barely twenty years old, the gifted young man began his public career in the fall of 1920 when he was invited to speak to a small group in a room over a bank in Santa Monica, California, on the subject of reincarnation. The following year, Hall was asked to hold a lecture program in Los Angeles; thereafter, he continued teaching and writing for another six decades. He showed thousands how "universal wisdom" could be found in the myths, mysteries, and symbols of the ancient Western mystery teachings and how to embody this wisdom in their own lives.

When a young student asked him to autograph one of his books, Hall wrote, "To learn is to live, to study is to grow, and growth is the measurement of life. The mind must be taught to think, the heart to feel, and the hands to labor. When these have been educated to their highest point, then is the time to offer them to the service of their fellow man, not before."

His book on Freemasonry explained that it was a structure built on experience. Each stone is a sequential step in the unfolding of intelligence. "The shrines of Masonry," he said, "are ornamented by the jewels of a thousand ages." Its rituals ring with the words of enlightened seers and illuminated sages. A hundred religions have brought their gifts of wisdom to its altar. Unnumbered arts and sciences have contributed to its symbolism. It is more than a faith; it is a path of certainty. "It was more than a belief," he said, "it is a fact."

> It is a university, teaching the liberal arts and sciences of the soul to all who will attend to its words. It is a shadow of the great Atlantean Mystery School, which stood with all its splendor in the ancient City of the Golden Gates, where now the turbulent Atlantic rolls in unbroken sweep. Its chairs are seats of learning; its pillars uphold the arch of universal education, not only in material things, but also in those qualities which are of the sprit.... Masonry is, in truth, that long-lost thing which all peoples have sought in all ages. Masonry is the common denominator as well as the common devisor of human aspiration.

Most of the religions of the world were like processions. One leads and many follow. In the footsteps of the demigods, man followed in his search for truth and illumination. Christians followed "the gentle Nazarene up the winding slopes of Calvary." The Buddhist followed his great emancipator through his wanderings in the wilderness. The Muslim "makes his pilgrimage across the desert sands to the black tent at Mecca." Truth leads. Ignorance follows in this train.

Spirit blazes the trail, and matter follows behind. In the world today ideals live but a moment in their purity, before the gathering hosts of darkness snuff out the gleaming spark. The Mystery School, however, remains unmoved. It does not bring its light to man; man must bring his light to it. Ideals, coming into the world, become idols within a few short hours, but man, entering the gate of the sanctuary, changes the idol back to an ideal. Man is climbing an endless flight of steps, with his eyes fixed upon the goal at the top. Many cannot see the goal, and only one or two steps are visible before them. He has learned, however, one great lesson—namely, that as he builds his own character he is given strength to climb the steps. Hence a Mason is a builder of the temple of character. He is the architect of a sublime mystery—the gleaming, glowing temple of his own soul. He realizes that he best serves God when he joins with the Great Architect in building more noble structures in the universe below. All who are attempting to attain mastery through constructive efforts are Masons at heart, regardless of religious sect or belief. A Mason is not necessarily a member of a lodge. In a broad sense, he is any person who daily tries to live the Masonic life, and to serve intelligently the needs of the Great Architect. The Masonic brother pledges himself to assist all other temple-builders in whatever extremity of life; and in so doing he pledges himself to every living thing, for they are all temple-builders, building more noble structures to the glory of the universal God. The true Masonic Lodge is a Mystery School, a place where candidates are taken out of the follies and foibles of the world and instructed in the mysteries of life, relationships, and the identity of that germ of spiritual essence within, which is, in truth, the Son of God, beloved of His Father. The Mason views life seriously, realizing that every wasted moment is a lost opportunity, and that Omnipotence is gained only through earnestness and endeavor. Above all other relationships he recognizes the universal brotherhood of every living thing. The symbol of the clasped hands, explained in the Lodge, reflects his attitude towards all the world, for he is the comrade of all created things. He realizes also that his spirit is a glowing, gleaming jewel which he must enshrine within a holy temple built by the labor of his hands, the meditation of his heart, and the aspiration of his soul.

Freemasonry was defined as "a philosophy which is essentially creedless." It is the truer for it. Its brothers bow to truth regardless of the bearer; they serve light, instead of wrangling over the one who brings it. In this way, they prove that they are seeking to know better the will and the dictates of the Invincible One. Hall said, "No truer religion exists than that of world comradeship and brotherhood, for the purpose of glorifying one God and building for Him a temple of constructive attitude and noble character."

After World War I, American Freemasonry began lobbying the federal government for federally funded public schools. In 1920, the Supreme Council Southern Jurisdiction, United States of America, Ancient and Accepted Scottish Rite, declared itself in favor of the creation of a Department of Education with a secretary in the president's cabinet. The Masonic historian Albert G. Mackey credited the Scottish Rite for "the passage of a federal educational bill that embodied the principle of federal aid to the public schools in order to provide funds for the equalization of educational opportunities to the children of the nation." Mackey said that when compulsory education became a reality, Masons were to encourage parents to make the schools so efficient "that their superiority over all other [parochial] schools shall be so obvious" that every parent will have to send his children to public schools.

In the 1920s, thirty-third-degree Mason Earl Warren (future U.S. Chief Justice) was Grand Master of the Grand Lodge of California. In his annual message to the brethren in California in 1936, he said that "the education of our youth can best be done, indeed it can only be done, by a system of free public education. It is for this reason that the Grand Lodge of California, ever striving as it does to replace the darkness with light, is so vitally interested in the public schools of our state.

By destroying prejudice and planting reason in its place it prepares the foundation of a liberty-loving people for free government."

Critics of Freemasonry have interpreted Warren's use of "prejudice" to mean parochial schools of the Catholic Church and that this reflected the fact that the Masonic order was not a mere social organization, but one composed "of all those who have banded themselves together to learn and apply the principles of mysticism and the occult rites." Christianity was being all but eradicated from the Craft. An anti-Mason author said it became "unthinkable to mention the name of Christ or to pray in the name of Jesus" and the Craft was set firmly on "universalism."

This was a point stressed by Hall. He wrote, "The true disciple of Masonry has given up forever the worship of personalities. With his greater insight, he realizes that all [religions] are of no importance to him compared to the life which is evolving within." He added that "the true Mason is not creed-bound. He realizes with the divine illumination of his lodge that as a Mason his religion must be universal: Christ, Buddha, or Mohammed, the name means little, for he recognizes only the light and not the bearer."

Those who saw Masonry as anti-Christian noted that Albert Pike had said in *Moral and Dogma* that Masonry "is the universal, eternal, immutable religion, such as God planted it in the heart of universal humanity."

Five years after Hall's book appeared, the world of Freemasonry was rocked by another book. Written by Cardinal José María Caro y Rodríguez, the archbishop of Santiago, Chile, the *Mystery of Freemasonry Unveiled* said that "in Masonry there are serious and sincere persons who are unaware of its objectives or of its works and who are not regulating their lives according to the influence of the Masonic doctrine and spirit." He stated that Masonry was a universal deception that "gains and holds its initiates, and indoctrinates deeply and at times forcibly regarding their real plans for the destruction of the Christian order, and the banishment of the very name of Christ, and even of God, all of which is proposed either openly or covertly, according to circumstances."

While intellectuals were analyzing Freemasonry, American lodges continued to shift from only an emphasis on the philosophical and religious aspects of the Craft to an organization devoted to public service and charity.

Presiding during the boom years of the mid- and late 1920s that Americans were happy to call "Coolidge Prosperity," Calvin Coolidge declared that "the business of America is business."

Freemasons who agreed with him included the automobile makers Henry Ford and Walter P. Chrysler. So did King Gillette, as his company sold countless razor blades. Other Masons who became American business tycoons were Alexander J. Horlick (inventor of malted milk), Eberhard Faber (pencil maker), James C. Penney (founder of the department store chain), and David Sarnoff (founder of the Radio Corporation of America and the National Broadcasting Company). Moviegoers flocked to see "pictures" made by Masons Cecil B. DeMille, Louis B. Mayer of Metro-Goldwyn Mayer, and Jack L. Warner, whose studio turned out a string of gangster films, and scores of others every week. Entertainers who belonged to the Craft ran the gamut from zany comics W. C. Fields, Harold Lloyd, and Oliver Hardy and Stanley Laurel to screen heartthrobs Clark Gable and Douglas Fairbanks. The country danced, sang along, and marched to the music of Irving Berlin, George M. Cohan, Louis Armstrong, Duke Ellington, Paul Whiteman, and John Philip Sousa. If they looked at government, they found Masons in Congress, seated on the Supreme Court, and ensconced in the White House.

The next president claimed by Freemasonry was Franklin D. Roosevelt. Born in Hyde Park, New York, on January 30, 1882, he attended Harvard and Columbia Law School. On St. Patrick's Day, 1905, he married Eleanor Roosevelt. Both were related to Theodore Roosevelt. Franklin served in several state and federal positions before being elected the governor of New York in 1928. In the summer of 1921, at age thirty-nine, he was stricken with polio. He received the three degrees in Masonry within Holland Lodge No. 8, New York City, in 1911. During his lifetime, he was supportive of Freemasonry and somewhat active in the fraternity. He was elected president in November 1932 to the first of four terms spanning the Great Depression and World War II.

When the Japanese attacked Pearl Harbor, Hawaii, on December 7, 1941, thousands of Masons who went off to battlefields around the world joined the ranks of Freemasons through history who had taken up arms, from the Crusader Knights Templar to the Doughboys who'd sailed to France in World War I in the belief they were defending not only Western civilization but also their Masonic brotherhood.

Chapter 13

Warrior Masons

IN DECEMBER 1941, FREEMASONS IN THE UNITED STATES FELT PROUD that Masons had been significant figures in every American war from George Washington leading the Continental army during the American Revolution to General John J. "Black Jack" Pershing as commander in chief of the American Expeditionary Force during World War I.

In that conflict, Eddie Rickenbacker became America's "Ace of Aces" by shooting down more than a score of German aircraft. An auto pioneer and racing champion before the war, he was chosen by Pershing to accompany him to France as his driver with the rank of sergeant, but press attention made it impractical to continue, so Brigadier General William Mitchell employed the champion driver to chauffeur him around France. Because Rickenbacker had gone to France to learn to fly, Mitchell grudgingly transferred him to flight training school to serve as an engineering officer. He was soon high in the air with devastating effect on the Germans. On September 14, 1918, he was promoted to captain and given the command of the Ninety-fourth Aero Squadron. On September 25, he registered his eighth and ninth kills within minutes of each other and earned the Medal of Honor. From October 15 to the end of the war on November 11, he earned the Distinguished Service Cross and nine Oak Leaf clusters for seventeen more confirmed combat victories. After the war, he pioneered civilian aviation, founded Eastern Airlines, and took his Masonic degrees in 1922 in Kilwinning Lodge No. 297, Detroit, Michigan, and his thirty-third degree in the Scottish

Rite in 1942. The Grand Lodge of New York gave him its Distinguished Achievement Medal.

During the rise to power of dictatorships in Germany, Italy, and Japan in the decades after the Great War, Rickenbacker and all American Masons observed with alarm that in all those countries Freemasonry was targeted as an enemy of the state. They knew that long before Adolf Hitler led the Nazi Party to power, he had publicly announced his plans for German conquest of Europe and world dominion in *Mein Kampf*. His autobiography, written while serving a prison sentence for attempting to overthrow the democratic government in Germany in the early 1920s, declared that Freemasonry had "succumbed" to Jews and had become an "excellent instrument" to fight for their aims and use their "strings" to pull the upper strata of society into their designs. "The general pacifistic paralysis of the national instinct of self-preservation," he said, had been instigated by Masons.

In 1931, Nazi Party officials were given a "Guide and Instructional Letter" that stated, "The natural hostility of the peasant against the Jews, and his hostility against the Freemason as a servant of the Jew, must be worked up to a frenzy."

The American Masonic historian Paul Bessel notes that when Hitler gained power legally, his deputy, Hermann Göring, summoned Grand Master Josias von Heeringen of the German Grand Lodge and told him there was no place for Freemasonry in Nazi Germany.

On August 8, 1935, *Völkischer Beobachter,* Hitler's newspaper, announced the final dissolution of all Masonic lodges in Germany and blamed Freemasonry for events in Sarajevo in 1914 that led to World War I. Paul von Hindenburg, the German president, issued a decree charging the Masonic lodges had engaged in subversive activities. The minister of the interior ordered their immediate disbandment and confiscation of the property of all lodges.

A decade before, the Italian dictator Benito Mussolini's fascist council decided that fascists who were Freemasons had to choose between the two. The Masonic Grand Orient replied that fascist Freemasons were at liberty to give up Masonry and that such action "would be in accord with the love of country which is taught in the lodge." Many

Masons resigned and a period of violence against Masons and destruction of their property broke loose. Grand Master Domizo Torrigiani appealed to Mussolini about this violence, but the response was a declaration in August 1924 that fascists must disclose the names of Freemasons who were not in sympathy with the fascist government. Committees were appointed to collect information about Freemasonry. In 1925, Mussolini gave an interview in which he said that while Freemasonry in England, the United States, and Germany was a charitable and philanthropic institution, in Italy it was deemed a political organization that was subservient to the Grand Orient of France. Most lodges ceased meeting, but the Italian Grand Orient continued through 1925. Mussolini then charged Italian Freemasons with being agents for France and England and opponents of Italy's military actions. The persecution increased, with many prominent Freemasons assassinated. In January 1926, the government appropriated the already looted Grand Orient building.

In Japan, Masonry was considered "secret and subversive." Japanese were forbidden to enter or organize any secret society, fraternity, or institution. By the spring of 1940, Masonic activity in Japan had slowed considerably. Many members had left the country. In the summer of 1941 as the United States and Japan froze each others' assets, articles were published warning Masons to get out of the country.

As Japan invaded China, assisting the Chinese in desperately defending themselves was an American. A member of League City Lodge No. 1053, League City, Texas, the aviator Claire Lee Chennault was born in Commerce, Texas, on September 6, 1890. At age five, he relocated with his family to Louisiana. A descendant from eighteenth-century Huguenot immigrants and related to Sam Houston on his mother's side and Robert E. Lee on his father's side, he had a short temper that resulted in charges of insubordination and unorthodox ideas that forced him to retire from the army in 1937. Several months later, he was hired as a civilian consultant to the Chinese leader Generalissimo Chiang Kai-shek. For two years, he taught Chinese pilots and fought the Japanese from a base at Kunming. It took Chennault a long time to convince Chinese pilots that their lives were more important than saving face. They simply refused to bail out of a crippled plane because returning without their planes would cause their families embarrassment.

In October 1940, approximately one year before Japan attacked Pearl Harbor, Chennault proposed American air strikes against the Japanese. These would be covert operations against a country with which the United States still had peaceful diplomatic relations. The bombing missions were to be carried out by American mecenaries paid by the American government through a private corporation. This newly formed unit, a covert entity of the Office of Strategic Services, was given the name "American Volunteer Group." It was to fly American planes (Curtis Warhawk P-40s) painted with Chinese insignias. The unit later became known as the "Flying Tigers." On April 15, 1941, President Roosevelt signed an executive order permitting members of the U.S. Navy, Marine Corps, and Army Air Corps to resign from their branch of service with the assurance that they would be reinstated to their former rank or grade following completion of their contract. Since the United States was technically at peace with Japan, the plan required some subterfuge. On July 23, 1941, Roosevelt formally authorized Chennault's air strikes against the Japanese. They became the first Americans to see action against the Japanese. Relatively small in number, the planes were occasionally repainted different colors to fool the enemy into thinking the force was much larger than it actually was. Chennault was a thirty-second degree, a knight commander of the Court of Honour, Orient of China at Shanghai (in exile), and a noble of Islam Shrine Temple, San Francisco.

The next American flier and Mason to bring the war to Japan was James Harold "Jimmy" Doolittle. A member of the Hollenbeck Lodge No. 319, Los Angeles, California, he led a fleet of B-25 bombers in a raid on Tokyo and other Japanese cities. They took off from the tightly packed deck of the aircraft carrier U.S.S. *Hornet* on April 18, 1942, the anniversary of Paul Revere's famous ride warning of a British march to Lexington and Concord in 1775. Doolittle's bombs inflicted little damage, but sent American morale soaring and made Doolittle a national hero. He led the air force in bombing raids in the skies over Europe.

Chosen by Roosevelt as overall commander of U.S. forces, General George C. Marshall was made a Mason on sight by Washington Lodge

No. 177. General Douglas MacArthur, who was also initiated on sight, commanded the Rainbow Division in France during the World War I and was based in the Philippines on December 7, 1941. Ordered to leave the islands by Roosevelt to command the army in the Pacific theater, he pledged to those who remained behind, "I shall return." He later said of the Craft, "Freemasonry embraces the highest moral laws and will bear the test of any system of ethics or philosophy ever promulgated for the uplift of man."

Omar N. Bradley, the U.S. Army commander under General Dwight D. Eisenhower (not a Mason) on D day, June 6, 1944, and throughout the European campaign, entered Masonry at West Point Lodge No. 877. Henry "Hap" Arnold, the commander of U.S. air forces, was raised a Mason in Junction City, Kansas, in 1927 and took Scottish Rite degrees at Leavenworth, Kansas, in 1929. He attained thirty-third degree in 1945. Fleet Admiral Ernest J. King joined Masonry in George C. Whiting Lodge No. 22, Washington., D.C. (now Potomac Lodge No. 5), in 1935. He attained the Royal Arch degree in San Diego, California, in 1938 and was a member of the Knights Templar Commandery in Cleveland, Ohio.

Six of seven army and air force four- or five-star generals and one of four fleet admirals in U.S. history were Masons.

Left in command of American and Filipino forces after MacArthur's departure, General Jonathan Wainwright and his tiny garrison held on bravely at Corregidor and were imprisoned for more than three years. Liberated from a prisoner-of-war camp two days before the Japanese surrender, Wainwright was flown to Tokyo to stand beside MacArthur during the surrender ceremony aboard the battleship U.S.S *Missouri*. Awarded the Congressional Medal of Honor, he took all three Masonic degrees in 1946 and was elevated to the thirty-second degree of the Scottish Rite Mason at the Shrine in Salina, Kansas. He died in 1953 and was interred in Arlington National Cemetery with Masonic honors.

The most famous recipient of the Medal of Honor for gallantry in World War II was the young Texan Audie Murphy. The most decorated soldier of the war, he went from private to commander, Company B, Fifteenth Infantry Regiment, Third Infantry Division, that fought from

Italy through southern France. Wounded in January 1945, he returned home, and on the basis of his fame and boyish looks he became a movie star. When his life story was made into a film, which was based on his autobiography *To Hell and Back,* he portrayed himself. He was inducted into the Craft at the North Hollywood Lodge No. 542 and received the thirty-second degree in Dallas, Texas. A successful businessman after retiring from films, he was killed in a plane crash on May 28, 1971.

Other Masons who were awarded the Medal of Honor during World War II were:

William Shomo, Major U.S. Army Air Corps. On January 11, 1945, on a strafing and photo reconnaissance mission during assault landings on Luzon in the Philippines, he encountered an enemy bomber and twelve fighter planes. He attacked and shot down six fighters and the bomber while his wingman took out three more. This give him the distinction of becoming an ace in a day. He was master Mason of Dormont Lodge No. 684, Pennsylvania.

Sergeant Hulon Whittington, U.S. Army. At Grimenil, France, July 29, 1944, he took over command of his platoon when his platoon leader and the platoon sergeant became casualties. He mounted a tank and through the turret directed fire on an advancing column of German Mark V tanks and then led a bayonet charge. When a medic was wounded, Whittington administered first aid to his wounded men. He was a member of Oak Harbor Lodge No. 495, Oak Harbor, Ohio.

When the United States entered World War II on December 8, 1941, Robert J. Dole of Russell, Kansas, was in his second year of college. He left to enlist in the army and became a member of the Tenth Mountain Division. Leading an attack on a German machine gun nest in Italy's Po Valley on April 14, 1945, he was hit by shrapnel from an exploding shell. His right hand was almost gone. Several neck and spinal vertebrae were fractured. Shell fragments had penetrated much of his body. Three years of hospitalization and three operations followed. He slowly recovered the ability to stand, walk, and use his left arm and hand. He married Elizabeth Hanford of Raleigh, North Carolina. In 1950, he was elected to the Kansas legislature and later served as a Russell County attorney. He was elected to the U.S. House of Representative in 1960 and was reelected in 1962, 1964, and 1966. He then moved to the U.S. Senate in 1968 and was reelected in 1974, 1980, 1986, and 1992. In 1976, he was the unsuccessful Republican candidate for vice president on a ticket with President Gerald Ford. His career in the U.S. House and Senate includes service as a member of the House and Senate committees on agriculture and chair of the Senate Finance Committee. In 1984, he was elected Senate majority leader. He served four consecutive Congresses as Senate Republican leader, until he retired from the Senate in 1996 to seek the Republican nomination for the presidency and lost.

Dole entered Masonry at Russell Lodge No. 177 on April 19, 1955, rose to Fellowcraft on June 7, and Master on September 20, 1955. He completed Scottish Rite degrees in the Valley of Salina on December 10, 1966, and York Rite in Aleppo Commandery No. 31, Hays, Kansas.

American Freemasons who could not go off to combat took part in the Masonic Service Association. Its centers offered dancing, singing, and food. "To a lonely soldier, sailor, or marine," said a Masonic historian, "the centers often provided the last touch of home before they went overseas. Just reading the old records from this period of time makes one proud to be a Mason." After World War II, the need for the service centers was gone, but more than 20 million military personnel, sick, maimed, and injured needed care. The government formed the Veterans Administration and the Veterans Administration Voluntary Service. This provided Masonic lodges a means to aid veterans. The Masonic Service Association notes that members do 250,000 volunteer hours per year. One of these volunteers was the subject of a story in the *Capital Times* in Madison, Wisconsin, on Christmas Day, 2001:

> John Hendrickson of rural Verona, Wisconsin was a prisoner of war during World War II, and he remembers Christmas 1944 as the holiday when he was marched across Germany with other POW's. It

was the coldest winter in Germany's history. On Christmas Eve he was temporarily locked with other POW's in a boxcar of a train that came under attack by Allied forces.

"When the planes started firing our German guards fled, and we were sitting ducks," he recalls.

After Hendrickson and the others were able to get out of the box-car, they used their bodies to form the word "POW" in the snow. The "friendly fire" stopped.

"There was an angel watching over us that day," Hendrickson says.

These war memories surface occasionally, but Hendrickson, now 82, would rather talk about his work as a volunteer at the Middleton Memorial Veterans Hospital in Madison, where he pours coffee, visits with patients and greets visitors four days a week.

"In 14 years, I have about 9,000 volunteer hours in," says Hendrickson, who is a member of the Masonic Service Association–Madison Chapter, an organization that helps to supply the Veterans Hospital with volunteers.

Before the Freemason warrior Theodore Roosevelt became assistant secretary of the navy and ordered the U.S. Navy to ready itself for war with Spain to liberate Cubans from Spain in 1898, Freemasons had been waging war for the island's freedom for decades as "filibusters." At that time, the term did not have its present meaning as a device in the U.S. Senate to delay or block legislative action and presidential appointments to the Supreme Court and other posts. In 1898, a filibuster was a form of illegal naval action by private Americans, with Freemasons taking a prominent role, to harass the rulers of the Spanish colony and aid Cuban revolutionaries.

As chronicled in the 1997 essay "Filibusters and Freemasons: The Sworn Obligation" in the *Journal of the Early Republic*, Antonio de la Cova notes that from 1848 to 1851, Cuban separatists in the United States established organizations, released publications, and mustered four filibuster invasions to overthrow the Spanish colonial government and establish a Cuban republic. They followed the example of Texans in their struggle with Mexico by using American funds, volunteers, and weapons to achieve independence.

"Filibuster expeditions led by disgruntled former Spanish Army General Narciso López and his aide-de-camp Ambrosio José Gonzales," writes de la Cova, "violated the Neutrality Law of 1818, prohibiting armed enterprises against nations at peace with the United States. López's attempts to liberate Cuba had profound consequences for United States–Spanish relations and the course of Cuban history."

López, Gonzales, and most of the filibuster leadership were Freemasons who relied extensively on the international fraternity to accomplish their plans. There had been similar precedent in the creation of the Republic of West Florida in 1810 and the Republic of Texas in 1836. Louisiana Freemasons led the revolt against Spain that proclaimed the seventy-two-day Republic of West Florida, an area that was later annexed to the state.

The de la Cova essay contends that secret Masonic identification facilitated joining the filibuster organization and provided protection from federal authorities seeking to suppress their activities. Freemasonry espoused an intellectual rationale justifying the invasion of Cuba and Masonic doctrine emphasized that tyranny was the enemy of the human race.

One writer notes that one filibuster had joined the fraternity in Spain and later belonged to Solomon's Lodge No. 1, Savannah, Georgia. Filibuster leaders Cirilo Villaverde and Henry Theodore Titus were members of a lodge in Jacksonville, Florida.

The first conspiracy for Cuban independence occurred in 1810 in the Theological Virtues Lodge No. 103, Havana. Three members, Román de la Luz, Luis F. Bassave, and Joaquín Infante, were charged with "attempted insurrection" and deported to Spain. In 1823, Cuban Freemasons created the clandestine independence movement Soles y Rayos de Bolívar. They sent a delegation of six brethren to meet with the liberator and Freemason Simón Bolívar in Colombia and with Mexican independence leaders who belonged to the fraternity. Requesting help to overthrow the colonial government, the group included twenty-year-old Gaspar Betancourt Cisneros, who later figured prominently in the filibuster

movement. Bolívar told the Cuban delegation that the moment was not
"ripe" for their plans. The following year, King Ferdinand VII, who had
been deposed by Masonic military officers in 1820, returned to power in
Spain and ordered Freemasons to cease or be summarily hanged for
treason. The fraternity went underground in Spain and Cuba and was
subjected to new persecutions in 1848, including property confiscations
and exile banishments.

A group of Cuban Freemasons and former independence conspirators created the Havana Club in the spring of 1848. Its members, de la
Cova notes, were mainly aristocrats and sugar planters, some of whom
partly feared that the abolitionist policies being pressured on Spain by
England and France would ruin Cuba's sugar economy.

> The organization agreed to hire five thousand American Mexican
> War veterans to invade and overthrow the regime. At the same time,
> another separatist conspiracy, led by General Narciso López, had been
> brewing in the central Trinidad region of Cuba. López had risen to
> prominence in Spain during a revolt of Liberal and Masonic army
> officers. When the conspiracy was discovered on July 4, 1848,
> López fled to the United States. The following month, the Havana
> Club sent Ambrosio José Gonzales, a twenty-nine-year-old college
> professor educated in New York City, to propose their invasion
> plan to a U.S. General and Mexican War hero William Jenkins
> Worth. They greeted each other with a Masonic secret-grip. Gonzales
> offered Worth three million dollars, of which one hundred thousand
> would be for himself, to invade Cuba with five thousand American
> volunteers. Worth accepted the proposition and invited the Cuban
> to accompany him to his hometown of Hudson, New York. He took
> Gonzales to West Point, and introduced him to Professor Gustavus
> Woodson Smith, a Freemason, and other army officers sympathetic
> to Cuban liberty.

Before the plot was realized, the War Department transferred Worth
to Texas, where he died of cholera shortly after his arrival. The Cubans
then offered the leadership of the expedition to the Mexican War vet-

eran General Caleb Cushing, a Freemason and former Massachusetts Whig Representative. In December 1848, Cushing introduced Gonzales to President James K. Polk and members of his cabinet. Cushing was forced to return to Massachusetts because of his father's terminal illness and declined to join the Cuban expedition. Gonzales stayed in the capital and met politicians sympathetic to the Cuban cause, including northern Democratic senators Stephen Douglas of Illinois and Daniel Dickinson of New York. Dickinson and Douglas were prominent Freemasons.

De la Cova states:

> Gonzales returned to New York City, where in June 1849 he participated in a Cuban conspiratorial meeting in a boarding house with López and his followers. They incorporated Masonic emblems in the design of their flag and agreed to use red, white and blue tricolor of liberty. Master Mason Miguel Teurbe Tolón drew three oblong horizontal blue stripes, separated by two white stripes, to represent the three regions into which Spain divided Cuba. López superimposed on the banner's left an equilateral triangle, resembling a Master Mason's apron, "for besides its Masonic significance it is also a striking geometrical figure."

He rejected placing the Masonic all-seeing eye in the center of the triangle because it was difficult to embroider. They used the five-pointed star of the Texas flag because it also carried a symbolic meaning.

In early July 1849, recruitment for the invasion of Cuba was openly promoted in New York, Boston, Baltimore, and New Orleans. About 400 unarmed filibusters, including many Mexican War veterans, departed New Orleans and assembled on Round Island, three miles south of Pascagoula, Mississippi. When President Zachary Taylor learned of these events, he issued a proclamation on August 11 against the "criminal" invasion of Cuba and ordered the navy to blockade the island. During the next two months, the plotters were allowed to disperse. Two months later, Gonzales met John Henderson at a White House party (December 21, 1849). A former Mississippi Whig senator, a brigadier general of the state militia, and a Freemason, Henderson was a political ally of the Mississippi governor John Quitman and had played "a great part" in Texas annexation. Henderson invited the Cuban revolutionaries to move their base of operations to New Orleans, where Henderson kept a law office.

López went to reside in the home of the attorney Laurent Sigur, the editor of the *New Orleans Delta,* whose father had been the founding worshipful master of Perfect Union Lodge No. 1, the first Masonic temple established in Louisiana (1794). Henderson also introduced López and Gonzales to John Quitman in Jackson, Mississippi, on March 15, 1850. The visitors exchanged the Masonic greeting with their hosts. The governor, who is regarded as the "father of Mississippi Masonry," became a master Mason in Hiram Lodge No. 18, Delaware, Ohio, in 1820. He was the grand sovereign of the Southwest, the grand inspector general of the thirty-third degree of the Southern Division of the United States of Mississippi, and was a founder of the Supreme Council. He was also an honorary member of the Grand Lodge of South Carolina and of the grand lodge in his native New York. Quitman had been elected Grand Master of his state from 1826 to 1838, guiding the fraternity through the turbulent anti-Masonic era.

Also attending the meeting with the Cubans were three justices of the Mississippi High Court of Errors and Appeals, Chief Justice William L. Sharkey, Judge Cotesworth Pinckney Smith, and Judge Samuel S. Boyd. The first two were Freemasons. Sharkey was made a Master Mason in 1825 in Washington Lodge No. 3. The judges gave legal opinions on circumventing the federal Neutrality Law. Quitman concluded that after the Cuban people revolted, he would resign as governor and lead an expedition to reinforce López. He agreed to meet the Cubans in New Orleans in a fortnight for a secret purpose. Freemasons occupied the highest positions in the military command structure.

General Jean Baptiste Donatien Augustin, the commander of the Louisiana Legion, a state militia regiment, provided most of the weapons. The state of Mississippi provided fifty Yager model "Mississippi" rifles, which were loaded on board the expedition vessels before they sailed out of New Orleans. López and 521 expeditionaries landed in Cárdenas, Cuba, in the early hours of May 19 and captured the town after a skirmish with Spanish troops, resulting in three filibusters killed and nine wounded, including Gonzales. The populace failed to join the mainly English-speaking invaders. A Spanish counterattack that afternoon resulted in fifteen expeditionaries killed and nineteen wounded.

Other filibusters followed, but were thwarted by the U.S. government. Some of the Masons were imprisoned but others were celebrated as heroes. In one instance, John Hardee Dilworth, a government official and Freemason, said to one of the wanted filibusters, "It so happens that I have an order for your arrest from the President of the United States. I am most happy to make your acquaintance and to welcome you to my house. I sympathize deeply with your cause."

Historians speculate that Freemasons were motivated to assist the independence movement because they recalled the anti-Masonic era in the United States and sympathized with the Cubans. They were also motivated by their fraternal doctrine against tyranny, regarding themselves in a similar role as America's Masonic Founding Fathers. De la Cova believes that Masons were a main ingredient of the filibuster movement because of their sworn Masonic obligation to grant relief to a worthy distressed brother no matter who or where he was. "Freemasonry alone did not create the American, Texas and Cuban revolutions," de la Cova writes, "but it did prepare and accomplish them."

A review on an Internet Web site of Freemasonry's historic and intimate connections to the military notes that when the United States was drawn into World War II after the Japanese sneak attack on December 7, 1941, Masonic lodges across the country were swamped with applications for membership. The article asks: "Why was it so important to these men to join before they went into battle?"

The provided answer is that they knew if they were killed, there would be help for their widows and children. Masons take care of their wives, widows and orphans. But they also knew that anywhere in the world they might be, even in a hostile country, they would find friends and brothers. This is still true. It is also true that you'll find in Freemasonry something else that's found in the military—men who understand what it means to live lives of honor and integrity; men who won't leave you to face the enemy, or the world, by yourself.

The item continued, "It's been a long time since warriors went into battle on horseback, armed with lance and battle-axe, and it's been a long time since Masons built castles. The tools of both have changed, but the spirit hasn't."

Freemasonry attempts to cultivate that spirit in a youth organization that is named for the martyr of the romanticized and mysterious ancient order of Knights Templar.

Chapter 14

Sons of the Templars

NEAR THE CLOSE OF WORLD WAR I IN 1918, FRANK SHERMAN Land, an Illinois businessman, grew concerned with problems of boys who had lost their fathers. He recalled thinking "how lonely it must be for a boy not to have a man to talk with, or a man to provide some type of inspiration and direction." A Freemason, he decided that there was a need for some kind of organization in which boys would have an opportunity to associate with other boys, share their common interests, and learn responsibility and other beneficial skills from professional men like himself who were also Masons and able to befriend, advise, and even provide jobs.

In March 1919, Land met with Louis Lower Jr., whose father had died. Land took the time to talk to Lower. He asked the boy to invite a few friends to a meeting. Lower brought eight: Ivan M. Bentley, Edmund Marshall, Gorman A. McBride, Jerome Jacobson, William W. Steinhilber, Elmer Dorsey, Clyde C. Stream, and Ralph Sewell. This resulted in a second group of thirty-one. Excited about their new "club," they wanted to name it. Land told them the story of a thirteenth-century martyr of the Order of Knights Templar.

According to Masonic history, in 1298 Jacques de Molay was named grand master of the Knights Templar. It was a time in which the Christian Crusades were failing in their goal of securing the Holy Land. Islamic Saracens had defeated other Crusaders, leaving the Templars and another order, the Hospitalers, to confront the "infidels." To reorganize and regain their strength, the Templars traveled to the island of Cyprus and waited for the general public to rise up in support of another Crusade. What they encountered was enmity among powerful lords who were interested in only obtaining wealth and power. In 1305, the king of France, Philip the Fair, set about to gain control of the Knights Templar. Until then, they had been accountable only to the Catholic Church. By doing so, Philip hoped to checkmate the pope and increase his own wealth.

In 1307, Philip had de Molay and hundreds of Knights Templar seized and put in prison. For seven years, they suffered torture and inhuman conditions. Philip then managed to force Pope Clement V to condemn the Templars. Their wealth and property were confiscated and given to Philip's supporters. During these years of torture, de Molay continued to be loyal to his friends and knights. He refused to disclose the location of the order's funds and to betray his comrades. On March 18, 1314, he was tried by a special court that heard a forged confession bearing de Molay's signature. He disavowed it. Under the laws of the time, the disavowal of a confession was punishable by death. Another Knight Templar, Guy of Auvergne, also disavowed his confession. Both were burned at the stake.

The account of these events cited in the *Catholic Encyclopedia* differs dramatically. It notes that de Molay was born in Rahon, Jura, in about 1244. A Templar since 1265 and a grand master of the templars as early as 1298, de Molay is said to have described himself at his trial as an unlettered soldier (*miles illetteratus*). He presided in 1306 or 1307 at the drawing up of a very important "plan of crusade" and went to Poitiers, France, to lay it before Pope Clement V. This project, based on personal knowledge of the Orient and the Italian cities, was considered to be superior to any other Crusade of its kind. In it, de Molay showed his implicit confidence in the king of France, but learning from Clement V that accusations had been brought by Philip against the Templars, de Molay "begged the pope to do justice" and returned to Paris. On Friday, Ocotber 13, 1307, he was arrested with all the Templars at their central house in Paris. Questioned by the king's lawyer, de Molay knew neither law nor theology and was not able defend himself. In his first appearance before the inquisitor general on October 24, 1307, he pleaded guilty to some of the charges, including an alleged obligation of the Templars to deny Christ and to spit on the crucifix when joining the order. He refused to admit to crimes against chastity (sodomy). He gave the same admissions and denials the following day.

"It is supposed that his object in making these partial admissions," says the *Catholic Encyclopedia*, "was to save his comrades from the extreme penalty [of death]."

In 1308, a commission of inquiry of eight cardinals was appointed by the pope. It was a new form of procedure, in that it excluded torture. De Molay "caused to be surreptitiously circulated in some of the dungeons a wax tablet calling upon his brethren to retract their confessions." He appeared before this commission in August 1308. According to the record of his trial in the bull of Clement V, *Faciens misericordiam*, de Molay "would seem to have repeated his admissions of guilt." When the bull was read to de Molay before another commission in November 1309, de Molay made the sign of the cross twice and exclaimed, "Would to God that such scoundrels might receive the treatment they receive from the Saracens and Tartars!"

From this account, it appears that the cardinals of the 1308 commission attributed to de Molay admissions he had not made to save him from the wrath of King Philip. From motives of "humanity," they created a lie to save him. "Before this commission of 1309," the encyclopedia continues, "[de] Molay displayed true courage. When they spoke to him of the sodomy of the Templars, and of their transgressions against religious law, he answered that he had never heard of anything of the kind, and asked permission to hear Mass." The trial dragged on. In March 1313, de Molay and three other dignitaries of the order underwent a final interrogatory in Paris before another commission of cardinals, prelates, and theologians, who were authorized to pronounce sentence. De Molay was condemned to imprisonment for life. Still proudly denying the crimes with which the Templars had been charged, he was judged "relapsed" by Philip the Fair and burned at the stake in the shadow of the Notre Dame Cathedral.

According to legend, as the flames engulfed de Molay, he prophesied that Philip and Pope Clement V would die within the year. They did.

Reportedly, de Molay's final words were "*Vekam, Adonai!*" ("Revenge, O Lord!" in the Hebrew language).

The group of Freemasons that Land founded to help boys in 1919 became the Order of DeMolay, and it consisted of young men between the ages of fourteen and twenty-one. As interest in DeMolay spread, Land answered many requests for information and authority to start chapters. Initiations and ceremonies took place on all locations. By the fall of 1920, the "mother chapter" had developed activities for its members as well, including a baseball team, a DeMolay marching unit, and a 100-piece band. By the end of 1921, Land realized he was giving all his time to the new organization and that he had become a full-time DeMolay employee. As DeMolay chapters grew in numbers and strength, the organization grew in prestige. With this greater recognition, interest developed in the Masonic fraternity. Official recognition and approval by Masonic groups came when they began giving their seal of approval to foster DeMolay in their states. Many distinguished organizations endorsed DeMolay, including the Generals Grand Chapter of Royal Arch Masons, grand lodges, and Knights Templar. Land became a figure of international prominence within Masonry, eventually becoming imperial potentate of the Shrine of North America. He counted among his friends U.S. congressmen, state governors, movie and radio stars, military leaders, titans of industry, and U.S. presidents.

Among members claimed by DeMolay are President Bill Clinton; news broadcasters Walter Cronkite, Dan Rather, and Paul Harvey; motion pictures' John Wayne, Walt Disney, Mel Blanc, and Buddy Ebsen; baseball player Pete Rose; football players Fran Tarkenton and Bob Mathias; folk singer Burl Ives; sports writer Red Barber; author John Steinbeck; and astronauts Frank Borman and Gordon Cooper.

Known as "Dad," as all senior DeMolays (over twenty-one) are called, Land worked for the Order of DeMolay until his death on November 8, 1959. The organization is in several countries around the world (18,000 chapters) with a total membership of more than a million. Each has the sponsorship of a Masonic lodge and cannot meet unless there is a Master Mason present. The ritual for the order was drawn up by the Scottish Rite Masons and covers seven points, including a pledge to live and think cleanly and to honor one's parents. DeMolay groups usually meet in Masonic temples and most become Masons when they are old enough.

A chapter of the International Order of DeMolay posted on its Web site the following Frequently Asked Question:

Q: What is the Order of DeMolay?

A: DeMolay is the world's largest fraternal youth organization. There are almost 2,000 Chapters in the U.S.A. and others in several foreign countries of the free world. The Order of DeMolay can provide a new, larger circle of friends, and it helps build character and leadership qualities.

Q: What do you do?

A: Chapters hold regular meetings. At these meetings various programs and activities are planned and discussed. Activities might include dances, parties, trips, maybe a camping trip, athletics such as basketball, softball, swimming, bowling, and just about any other type of activity. Everyone gets to participate in the planning, and everyone gets to play, regardless of ability. In short, a DeMolay Chapter can do whatever it sets its mind to do.

Q: What if school conflicts with DeMolay?

A: We stress that school comes first, and you are always excused if there is a conflict. There are more than enough activities for you to attend anyway, especially on weekends or during school breaks. Plus, DeMolay helps teach self-discipline, so it could help you to do better in school.

Q: I am involved in sports! Will I have time for DeMolay?

A: Our meetings usually start at about 7:30 P.M., so they are normally well after most practice sessions let out. You are always excused from DeMolay if there is a conflict. Besides, there are a lot of activities you can attend especially during the summer and off seasons.

Q: Isn't DeMolay a secret group?

A: Our principles and ideals are in no way secret. In fact, we want everyone to know what we stand for. The only "secrets" we have are things like handshakes, words and signs, so we are able to recognize other members, like many other groups.

Q: What is the Initiation like?

A: It is in two parts, both of which explain our general beliefs. The first part, called the Initiatory Degree, is a series of short talks, each about two minutes in length, explaining the Seven Cardinal Virtues of DeMolay: Love of Parents, Reverence for God, Courtesy, Comradeship, Fidelity, Cleanness in thought, word and deed, and Patriotism. The second part, called the DeMolay Degree, is a short play explaining why we named our organization after Jacques DeMolay, and teaches the important lessons of fidelity and loyalty.

A: What makes DeMolay different?

Q: There is a special feeling of closeness between DeMolays. When you join, the other members will actually be like brothers to you.

Q: Is DeMolay like a college fraternity?

A: It is in the sense that it is for young men, we hold initiations to bring in new members; but these initiations are of a serious nature. There are no stupid jokes played, and no hazing of any kind. If someone tells you that you "ride a goat" or get a "spanking," they are wrong.

Q: Aren't you a religious group?

A: No. DeMolay is a fraternal group. DeMolay does require a member to believe in God, but each member may worship as he sees fit. The Order of DeMolay encourages a boy to attend and participate in his Church or religious body. It does not support any denomination, nor does it denounce any denomination in any way. We require that you believe in God. What you believe about God is your business.

Q: What if I have work?

A: We understand that many boys have to work these days. We find that boys who work don't have much trouble getting off once in a while for some important DeMolay event or activity, especially when the employer finds out what type of organization DeMolay is. They become understanding when they learn about the ideals we teach. Also, there are a lot of employers who know about DeMolay, and being a DeMolay could actually help you get an even better job.

Q: What if I don't know many of the members?

A: Many join the Chapter without really being good friends to many members. After joining, you will find that the DeMolays often times become some of your best friends. You will know that you can count on them when you need them. Plus, why not get your friends to join DeMolay too?

Q: How much to join?

A: Our Chapter's fee for a Life Membership is only $100.00. Since this is a life membership fee, there are no yearly dues. If the initiation fee is a problem, we can always work out a time payment plan or something where you can join.

Q: How can I join?

A: Just fill out an application, which we call a Petition for Membership. Give it to a member of DeMolay or an Advisor. He will present it to the Chapter at the next meeting.

Q: Are there any girls in DeMolay?

A: None as members, but most Chapters have joint activities, such as dances with girls' organizations. Chapters also elect a Chapter Sweetheart each term of office, who is selected from a number of competitors who are nominated by a member of our Chapter. Many Chapter activities are of the nature where you will want to bring a date or you will meet a girl from the Order of Rainbow or Job's Daughters, which are girls' organizations.

The International Order of Job's Daughters was founded by Ethel T. Wead Mick in Omaha, Nebraska, in 1920. Its purpose is to band together girls between the ages of eleven to twenty with a Masonic relationship for the purpose of character building through moral and spiritual development. Their primary charity is the Hearing Impaired Kids' Endowment Fund, which provides hearing devices for children in need. The International Order of the Rainbow for Girls (ages eleven to twenty) with Masonic affiliations was founded by the Reverend W. Mark Sexson on April 6, 1922, in McAlester, Oklahoma.

The largest organization for women in Freemasonry is the Order of the Eastern Star. It was started by Dr. Robert Morris, a Master Mason and Past Grand Master of Kentucky. He intended the organization to become the female branch of Freemasonry, but men and women may belong.

Since the formation of the Grand Lodge of London in 1717 and the consolidation and refining of its rites and rituals in 1723 (known as the Anderson Constitutions, named for its author, James Anderson), women were not to be admitted to membership, in keeping with social customs and mores of that time. This was the rule for the rest of the eighteenth century and into the nineteenth century. In a study of women in Freemasonry, John P. Slifko of the University of California, Los Angeles, finds that the opening of the twentieth century saw significant attempts "to fashion a greater cosmopolitanism and internationalism."

This period witnessed the establishment of the Order of International Co-Freemasonry, Le Droit Humain, in France. In 1902 at a Geneva congress of thirty-four separate Masonic jurisdictions, the Bureau International des Relations Maçonniques was created, but it did not survive the war. However, notes Slifko, the perception of the need for close international and cross-jurisdictional relations in a "universal Freemasonry" was strong among women and men.

It appears that a women's lodge existed briefly in Boston in the 1790s. Its worshipful master, Hannah Mather Crocker, wrote a series of letters on Freemasonry that were published in Boston in 1815. She claims she had knowledge of the Craft because "in the younger part of life, [she] did investigate some of the principles of Free-Masonry" to assuage the fears of her friends whose husbands were Masons. She wrote that she "had the honor, some years ago, to preside as Mistress of a similar institution, consisting of females only; we held a regular lodge, founded on the original principles of true ancient freemasonry, so far as was consistent for the female character." Furthermore, there is a historical document that mentions "a short address by the Mistress of St. Ann's Lodge."

The most widely circulated story of a woman Mason in the United States is that of Catherine Babington, who lived in Kentucky in the 1800s. Masonic records note that near her house was a two-story building used by Masons as a lodge room. She is said to have concealed herself in the hollow pulpit at every meeting of the lodge for more than a year, seeing all the degrees and learning all the work. Finally discovered and "on being closely questioned," she showed "a remarkably proficient knowledge of the ritual." She was kept in custody for more than a month, and was eventually "obligated" but not admitted into the order.

A lodge that accepted women was formed in Philadelphia in 1778 by French officers in the Continental army. In the next century, Albert Pike, the supreme commander of Scottish Rite Freemasonry, created a Rite of Adoption based on the French ritual. One of the first women initiated into this Lodge of Adoption was the sculptor Vinnie Ream Hoxie, who created a statue of Abraham Lincoln displayed in the Rotunda of the U.S. Capitol.

In 1850, Dr. Robert Morris published a ritual under the name "The Rosary of the Eastern Star." Open to Freemasons and their female relatives, it was based partly on the French Adoptive Rite and partly on several orders in America that were likely based on the French order. Some of these early groups were Mason's Daughter, Mason's wife, Heroine of Jericho, and True Kindred. Morris conceived and arranged Star degrees. From 1865 to 1868, Macoy recast the ritual and organized the chapter system. The Macoy ritual is the foundation of the OES as it exists today. The OES claims a membership of more than 1 million members worldwide. Women in the Craft is called "co-Masonry."

In 1907, the American Federation of the Human Rights was incorporated in Washington, D.C. It soon had several lodges in the United States. Other co-Masonic bodies are George Washington Union and Grand Lodge Symbolic of Memphis-Misraïm. Four lodges created by the Women's Grand Lodge of Belgium since 1992 hope to form a Women's Grand Lodge of the United States.

The OES is a rite of Freemasonry with teachings based on the Bible and objectives that are "charitable and benevolent." Members must be eighteen years or older and be either master Masons in good standing or properly related to a Master Mason in good standing. The latter category includes wives, widows, sisters, daughters, grandmothers, granddaughters, and mothers and relatives by second marriage (stepmothers, stepdaughters, stepsisters, and half sisters). In 1994 this was expanded to include nieces and daughters-in-law.

Each chapter had eighteen officers, some elected and others appointed. Two offices are specifically male (Patron and Associate Patron). Nine offices are specifically female (including Matron and Associate Matron). While the Worthy Matron is considered to be the presiding officer of the chapter, the degrees cannot be conferred without a presiding brother who is in good standing. The chapter retains the right to decide who shall become a member. Election to the degrees must be unanimous, without debate, and secret. The successful candidate must profess a belief in a Supreme Being and is initiated in five degrees, which are conferred in one ceremony. (When the OES was created, it was intended to be the first of a three-degree series. The second and third degrees were Queen of the South and the Order of the Amaranth, respectively.) OES requires only a belief in a Supreme Being, even though the degrees are based in both the Old and New Testaments. While non-Christians are not specifically barred from membership, it would be difficult to be other than Christian and belong to the order.

In a study of the origin and history of the adoptive rite among black women, Jessie M. Ayers, Past Grand Worthy Matron of Miriam Chapter No. 4, OES, Georgiana Thomas Grand Chapter, Jurisdiction of the District, and Grand Historian of the Georgiana Thomas Grand Chapter, states that on August 10, 1874, "Thorton Andrew Jackson received the several degrees of the Rite of Adoption of the Order of the Eastern Star from C. B. Case, a deputy and agent of Illustrious Robert Macoy 33d degree Supreme Patron of the Rite of Adoption of the World." On December 1, 1874, Queen Esther Chapter No. 1, Order of the Eastern Star, was established at 707 O Street, NW, Washington, D.C., in the home of Georgiana Thomas. The first Worthy Matron was Sister Martha Welch and first Worthy Patron was Brother Thornton A. Jackson.

In December 1874, Grand Master William H. Myers and Deputy Grand Master William A. Tallaferro, Union Grand Lodge, Jurisdiction of the District of Columbia, were invited to receive the degrees. They both accepted, further cementing ties "that bind the Masonic Family together." Following the occasion of Grand Master Myers's initiation into the Adoptive Rite, Myers said, "May the dove of peace hover over you. May the All Seeing Eye, whom the Sun, Moon and Stars obey ever watch over you. May he keep and protect you in your every effort to promote interest in the general good of this chapter."

On April 29, 1890, Queen of Sheba Chapter No. 3, OES, was established, and on October 20, 1890, Gethsemane Chapter No. 4, OES, were formed by Jackson within the jurisdiction of the District of Columbia. He was also instrumental in establishing a chapter in Alexandria, Virginia, three chapters in Maryland, and three chapters in Pennsylvania.

During 1875, Pythagoras Lodge No. 9 presented the officers of Queen Esther Chapter No. 1 with their first badges, known as Rosettes. This presentation was by Jackson. He "admonished the officers to wear the Rosettes with dignity."

Ayres writes, "And so it was one hundred years after the founding of the first Black Lodge of Free and Accepted Masons, Queen Esther Chapter No. 1, Order of the Eastern Star, was officially instituted in the City of Washington in the District of Columbia."

A chapter of the OES provides the following Frequently Asked Questions on its Web site:

Q: Is the Order of the Eastern Star a secret society?

A: No. Secret societies are underground and hard to find. We are easily found within the community but we enjoy a distinctive means of identifying each other.

Q: Can I afford membership in the Order of the Eastern Star?

A: Financial position is not considered. Members come from all economic stations of life.

Q: Is my religious faith allowed in the Order of the Eastern Star?

A: Members of all religions may belong to the Order of the Eastern Star. We only require a belief in a Supreme Being.

Q: Is the order of the Eastern Star time consuming?

A: After your Initiation into our Order, you may attend as your time permits.

Q: Is there any memory work?

A: There is no mandatory memory work except the means of making yourself known if you wish to visit a Chapter or if you become an officer.

Q: Is the Order patriotic and democratic?

A: Members are taught an allegiance to preserve the good of their country.

The order has approximately 10,000 chapters in 20 countries and about 1 million members under its General Grand Chapter. The emblem is a five-pointed star. The character-building lessons taught in the order are stories inspired by female biblical figures. Its charitable foundation from 1986 to 2001 contributed $513,147 to research on Alzheimer's disease, juvenile diabetes, and juvenile asthma. It also provides financial aid to students of theology and religious music, as well as other scholarships. Many jurisdictions support a retirement center or nursing home for older members. Some homes are open to the public.

Charitable and humanitarian activities of the OES represent not only a shift in Freemasonry from a strictly masculine society for philosophical growth of its members but also its emergence as a significant public service group and charity in the United States.

Chapter 15

Only to Serve and Help

THE FIRST RECORDED ACT OF CHARITY IN AMERICAN MASONRY occurred on November 4, 1754. At the Lodge of Fredericksburg, Virginia, a petition from John Spottswood claiming that he was indigent was read. On a motion, he was given a pound, twelve shillings, and sixpence "to relieve his necessity." A famous Masonic poem by Lawrence N. Greenleaf, "The Lodge Room over Simpkins' Store," reads:

A widow's case—four helpless ones; Lodge funds were running low;
A dozen Brethren sprang to feet and offers were not slow;
Food, raiment, things of needful sort, while one gave a load of wood;
Another shoes for little ones, for each gave what he could.
Then spake the last: "I haven't things like these to give—but then,
Some ready money may help out."—and he laid down a ten.

In 1792, William Preston declared, "To relieve the distressed is a duty incumbent of all men, but particularly on Freemasons, who are linked together by an indissoluble chain of sincere affection. To soothe the unhappy, to sympathize with their misfortunes, to have compassion for their miseries, and to restore peace to their troubled minds, is the great aim we have in view. On this basis we form our friendships and our connections."

Not all such early efforts were so successful. From 1841 to 1857, the Grand Lodge of Missouri attempted to establish a Masonic college and failed. Other lodges also tried in Ohio, Kentucky, North Carolina,

Arkansas, and Georgia, but as one Masonic historian writes, maintaining higher education "proved more than Masons can do, and so they shifted their focus to serving the needs of others." The National Masonic Tuberculosis Sanatoria in Albuquerque, New Mexico, which was established in 1922, had to be closed because it encountered financial problems.

Today's American Masons proudly note that they provide medical and health services in the form of "American Masonic Philanthropy." These operations typically involve extensive physical plants and large capital investments. Among Masonic philanthropies are the Texas Scottish Rite Hospital for Children; the Scottish Rite Children's Medical Center in Georgia; Scottish Rite facilities for childhood speech and language, including learning disorders; the Knights Templar Eye Foundation; the Masonic Cancer Center at the University of Minnesota; and the Grotto Dentistry for the Handicapped Program.

Homes and orphanages are the oldest category of organized Masonic philanthropy. From its earliest beginnings, notes a 1997 report on the subject, "Freemasonry has admonished its members to provide support for widows and orphans, especially those of former Masons." This care was initially provided by local lodges, but it eventually came under the oversight of grand lodges as they began providing for their needy with centralized facilities. The first Masonic home in the United States was established by Kentucky Masons in 1866: the Masonic Widows and Orphans Home and Infirmary in Louisville, Kentucky. In 1927, the residents moved to a new facility in Masonic Home, Kentucky. Today, thirty-nine state grand lodges maintain homes, and eleven still have orphanages, though the need for the latter has diminished. Most grand lodges without homes care for their needy through various endowments that support them in outside facilities. The services provided in this category are generally available to Masons and their relatives, though some Masonic orphanages allow lodges to sponsor orphans unrelated to a Mason.

In the area of medical research, the Scottish Rite's activities include the Kansas Masonic Oncology Center, the Royal Arch Research Assistance Program (hearing), the Cryptic Masons Medical Research Foundation (arteriosclerosis research), the Masonic Medical Research Laboratory at Utica, New York (biomedical research), and the Indianapolis Scottish Rite Foundation (geriatric research at the University of Indiana Medical School). National charities given special support by Masonic organizations include the Muscular Dystrophy Association (Tall Cedars of Lebanon), the American Diabetes Association (Amaranth Diabetes Foundation), and the American Cancer Society, supported by the Eastern Star Cancer Research Project.

Masonic community activities include the annual Des Moines Masonic Christmas Day Dinner for anyone in the community, the Tennessee and Alabama Scottish Rite Shoe Programs for thousands of children who otherwise would attend school without proper shoes, the Ohio Special Olympics Summer Games for which every Special Olympian is supported by the Grand Lodge of Ohio, the Missouri and Kansas "Masonic Mile of Food" for the needy, and the Special Olympian division soapbox derby in Jamestown, New York. Masonic scholarships range from funds offered by thousands of local lodges to programs on a national basis. The Eastern Star Training has awards for religious leadership. The Illinois Scottish Rite Nursing Scholarship and the Knights Templar Educational Foundation provide low-cost education loans.

Georgia lodges were encouraged to participate in the "Secret Santa" program to assist needy families at Christmas by asking ministers of local churches to choose a struggling family with children to receive a secret visit from Masons. They leave gifts on the doorstep, knock on the door, and leave. Numerous lodges from coast to coast fingerprint and videotape children "should the unthinkable happen" and a child be abducted. In Rhode Island, a similar program, the Child Identification Program (CHIP), was started by Masons in partnership with police, the Rhode Island Dental Association, and the Rhode island Hygienist Association. They videotape, fingerprint, and take dental impressions of thousands of children around the state.

Masons in Charlton, Massachusetts, in conjunction with the police, offer a "Rape Aggression Defense System" to teach women self-defense. Masons help young people who have drug and alcohol problems through the National Masonic Foundation for the Prevention of Drug and Alcohol Abuse among Children, the Family of Masonry for the International Order of DeMolay, the International Order of Job's Daughters, and the International Order of Rainbow for Girls. Much of this activity is centered in Masonic buildings that have become local landmarks and tourist attractions. They include the Scottish Rite Supreme Council Museum and Library in Washington, D.C. (the first public library in the federal district); the George Washington Masonic National Memorial in Alexandria, Virginia; the Scottish Rite Masonic Museum of Our National Heritage in Lexington, Massachusetts; and the Masonic Memorial Auditorium and the Eastern Star's Peace Chapel at the International Peace Garden on the Manitoba–North Dakota Border. In 1986, Masons contributed $2 million toward the restoration of the Statue of Liberty. In 1997, Masons worked to help restore Fort McHenry in Baltimore, Maryland, the Memorial Arch dedicated to Washington at Valley Forge, Pennsylvania, and the Washington Monument in the national capital.

In 1995, North American Masonic philanthropies contributed $750 million, of which 90 percent went to the general public. Yet, as a Masonic historian observes, over the years, some tension has developed between Masons and their detractors about the propriety of Masonic philanthropy. Many anti-Masons accuse the fraternity of being little more than a mutual insurance society that teaches self-serving opportunism rather than true charity. Discussing the Craft's charitable work, Henry Wilson Coil in *Coil's Masonic Encyclopedia* warns, "There has been some disposition on the part of Masonic writers and orators to exaggerate on this subject and carry us into the higher realms of Christian love and sacrifice for the benefit of all mankind, as if a Masonic lodge were almost a monastery of friars sworn to poverty and universal benevolence."

The image of Freemasons as constantly altruistic and harmless appeared to have been shattered in March 2004 by an incident at a meeting of the Fellowcraft Club associated with Southside Masonic Lodge No. 493, Patchogue, New York. The club planned to initiate forty-seven-year-old William James in a ceremony that would test the initiate's nerve. With ten Masons present, James sat in a chair blindfolded.

Two tin cans were placed on a shelf by his head. Seventy-six-year-old Albert Eid stood twenty feet away to fire a handgun loaded with blanks (James, however, believed they were real bullets). A man standing behind James would knock the cans down with a stick as Eid "fired" at them. But Eid had two pistols. The one in his left pocket was a .22 caliber, and the gun in his right pocket was a .38 and loaded with real bullets. Drawing and firing the wrong one, he killed James.

A World War II veteran, Eid had a license to carry his own pistol, and he often did so. He pleaded not guilty to a charge of second-degree manslaughter and was released on $2,500 bail. Reporting that Eid "was wearing his blue Masonic jacket" at his arraignment in Central Islip and that the Suffolk County Police called the shooting an accident, "the consequence of one man's confusion," the *New York Times* added. "The fatality exposes this secret society, centuries old, to a rare degree of public scrutiny."

The article described police carrying "evidence and ritual objects out of the Masons' one-story lodge," while television reporters and curious neighbors examined "the club's bricked-over windows and peered into the front door to glimpse a bulletin board announcing the order's recent charity efforts." It continued:

> Masonic leaders statewide were quick to disavow the ritual and shooting, saying it was not Masonic custom to shoot guns at other members. Ron Steiner, a spokesman for the New York State Grand Lodge of Free and Accepted Masons, which oversees all Masonic lodges in the state, said the social club was not officially tied to the Masonic organization.
>
> "This is so far beyond the concept of reality it's mind-boggling," Mr. Steiner said. "I've never heard of anything like this."
>
> Mystery and suspicion are woven into the history of the Freemasons, who trace their roots to the stone workers' guilds that built medieval Gothic cathedrals. The guilds evolved into secret clubs over the years with secret handshakes and rituals, and symbols like an all-seeing eye, pyramid and compass. The Southside Masonic Lodge members developed their own initiation rituals for

the social club in the lodge that set them apart from most other Masonic organizations, members said. No members of the lodge could remember pistols being used in the rituals (they are not allowed inside Masonic clubhouses), but some described initiations that were part prank, part exercise in trust.

One member, Michael Paquette, said that when he was initiated into the group five years earlier, two mouse traps had been placed before him. He was told that one worked and one was broken. Another member tested the broken trap, then told Paquette to touch the "live one." He did and discovered that it was a dud. The purpose, he said, "was just for you to be there and realize you were in good hands, and you didn't have to fear anything."

"The Southside Masons are mostly middle-aged or retired men who come from middle-class backgrounds," the *Times* noted. "The group once included about 500 members, but membership here and at other Masonic lodges has fallen over the years, and the group now has about 150 members," said Peter Berg, a member. "There are about 67,000 Masons across New York State, and their numbers rose slightly last year, for the first time in a decade, Mr. Steiner said. Orders like the Southside Masons seem more concerned today with Christmas parties and raising money for blood drives and children's charities than ritual."

James had joined the Southside Masons in December 2003. Eid had been a member for more than thirty years and spent most of his free time at the lodge. James worked for the town of Brookhaven's Planning Department and was described as a friendly man who seemed deeply devoted to his family. His wife, Susan, said she had no idea what was happening at the Masons' lodge the night he was shot. "This is so very sudden, and I'm just very upset," she said outside the couple's home in Medford. "To me, it was just a social thing."

In January 2005, Eid was sentenced to five years' probation. He wept during the sentencing. Prosecutors took into account his acceptance of responsibility, remorse, lack of prior criminal history, and his record of military service in recommending probation.

Although news reports of the tragedy made it clear that the shooting had occurred at a meeting of a club, and not as part of the lodge's activities, to the majority of the public who had a vague impression that strange things took place in a Masonic lodge, it seemed a distinction without a difference. Unless a non-Mason took the time to seek more information from a Mason, the impression was that firearms and other weapons were integral to Masonic rituals. Although the rites of the three degrees reenact the murder of Hiram Abiff by apprentices in the building of King Solomon's Temple, at no stage in the ritual is the initiate in any danger, other than possible embarrassment if he makes a mistake.

Regarding clubs such as the one in which James was killed, the Masonic scholar Edward L. King writes that there are many consisting of lodge members whose primary purpose is to provide a clublike environment within the lodge building. They go under a variety of names: "Square & Compass Club," "Lunchtime Club," and "Fellowcraft Club," as in Patchogue.

King's article explains:

> In the 1950s and 1960s, such clubs were extremely popular, owing to the desire of men to find a place where they might enjoy friendly company either during the day or in the evening. Not wanting to frequent a bar, they could go to the Masonic lodge and enjoy a hearty game of cribbage (a true Masonic favorite!) and a non-alcoholic drink. Such clubs were especially attractive to widowers as they provided a friendly social environment to talk about most anything without fear of getting into a fight with a stranger. Most also raised funds for the Masonic Hall through card games with wives present, cribbage tournaments amongst the men, and more.

Most clubs had no initiation ceremony. All that was required was payment of club dues. A man who moved frequently might belong to several during his Masonic career. They were especially popular in some overseas locations where a small amount of membership dues from a large transient military population helped to provide friendship and fellowship that a traveling Freemason sought. As Masonry's membership declined in the 1970s and 1980s, such clubs seemed to fade away.

Only to Serve and Help

"Fun is fun," writes King, "but society has changed greatly and Freemasonry's family is changing with it, albeit perhaps found somewhat on the 'lagging edge.' Ways of doing things in the past do not resonate the same way as they once did. It is both hoped and likely that this horrid incident in the Masonic venue will cause many reevaluations leading to reconsideration and removal of all such vestiges of the past which ever cause another such hideous tragedy."

Because of the fatal shooting in a lodge, *The Da Vinci Code*, and *National Treasure*, the general public continues to perceive Freemasonry as being shrouded in mists of mystery and secrecy. But there is one aspect of Freemasonry that has never raised suspicion and fears. Everyone loves the Shriners.

Chapter 16

Freemasons and the Frat House

FOLLOWING A HISTORIC TRIP TO THE UNITED STATES IN THE 1830S that coincided with the rapid growth of American Freemasonry, the French aristocrat Alexis de Tocqueville noted in *Democracy in America* that Americans of all ages, conditions, and dispositions constantly formed associations, "They are the most fraternal people in the world."

Seventy years before Tocqueville, Thomas Jefferson, the primary author of the Declaration of Independence, had been a founding father of America's first college secret society. In 1750, Jefferson and several classmates started a group known as the Flat Hat Club (FHC; the name was inspired by their mortar board caps). Nearly three centuries later, its offspring are found on campuses from coast to coast, yet few members of today's campus fraternities are aware that they have Masonic roots. The first university secret society was organized at William and Mary College in colonial Virginia. It was a period that is described by historians as one in which education for the elite centered around the study of Greek and Latin. Electives were virtually unknown, and classic rather than current events dominated discussion. It was a difficult time for an adolescent, who was removed from the family and sent to college by parents to acquire discipline by being separated from "the corrosive influence of indulgent mothers" and receive a gentleman's education. Travel was difficult in these isolated settings and athletic and social events were few and far between. It was indeed all work and no play. But students had a way when there was a need to fulfill. The need was to be able to relax, to enjoy friendships and learn those things that can't be taught in the classroom, to put purpose and perspective into a personal way of life, and to belong.

In Williamsburg, Virginia, in 1750, the way to do this was to gather in the upper room of the Raleigh Tavern with college classmates from William and Mary. Over drinks, they talked, laughed, and called themselves the Flat Hat Club. These students didn't realize it, but they had organized the first general college fraternity. An editorial heralding the birth of FHC in the *Virginia Times-Dispatch* in 1775 commented on the importance of this association:

> If this society was that out of which Phi Beta Kappa grew, then the F.H.C. has the distinction of being the genesis, not alone of a great scholarly brotherhood, but likewise of the numberless Greek letter fraternities...that exert an immeasurable influence for the brotherhood of man. The discovery of the existence of this society is, therefore, of interest throughout the nation. It was most fitting therefore, that so ancient and honorable a name should have been given to the new publication at the College of William and Mary.

In a correspondence at the time, Jefferson said that the FHC was not for any useful purpose. The society may have been purely social. But a list of books in the possession of the society includes such authors as John Locke, Isaac Newton, Joseph Priestly, Benjamin Franklin, Edmund Halley, David Hume, and Horace Walpole. The badge of the club was circular with an elaborate coat of arms on one side, and FHC on the other.

Beneath was the date and motto:

Nov. XI. MDCCL
Stabilitas et Fides

Similar groups sprouted. When one of these rejected a student who was a superior, John Heath, the rejected party, and four friends held the first secret meeting of Phi Beta Kappa, the first Greek letter society, on

December 5, 1776. These groups had to remain secret because at the time the William and Mary faculty didn't approve of its students discussing the pressing issues of the day—such discussions would cause them to lose focus on the classics. As such, Phi Beta Kappa developed secret signals of challenge and recognition as its members convened weekly in the Raleigh Tavern's Apollo Room. The secret group had mottos, rituals, and a distinctive badge that were inspired by and copied from the rites and the ritual of Freemasonry. The group also had secret meetings and initiations, pledges of loyalty and secrecy, special handshakes, signs, symbols, and jewelry in the form of badges, rings, and pins.

In a time when Freemasonry was rapidly growing and acting hand in hand with those in the leadership for American independence, the precepts of Masonry would be adapted by the fraternal movement in colleges. When Phi Beta Kappa felt that other college campuses should share its idea that the higher-education experience give proper consideration to the pressure on the student for future responsibilities by preparing him socially, chapters were founded at Harvard and Yale in 1779. Others soon followed. Meanwhile, Phi Beta Kappa became purely intellectual in its aims, though the original cardinal principles were "literature" and the Masonic goals were "morality and friendship."

Following the scandal involving the murder of William Morgan by Masons in 1826, the country was swept up in a backlash against secret societies in general and Masonry in particular. During this antisecret organization movement, Phi Beta Kappa voluntarily revealed that its name meant "Philosophy, the Guide of Life." Since then, it has become a scholastic honorary society and today recognizes undergraduate men and women who show superior achievements in academics. Its symbol is a small gold key. In 1812, four members of Phi Beta Kappa at the University of North Carolina formed Kappa Alpha, which quickly expanded to more than twenty campuses throughout the South. It didn't survive the Civil War. In the North, the decline of a military marching club in Union College (Schenectady, New York) left a void in student life in the fall of 1825. Consequently, a group of students, including several members of Phi Beta Kappa, organized Kappa Alpha Society on

November 26, 1825. Kappa Alpha Society claimed the distinction of being the first Greek letter general college fraternity with continuous existence to date. Because of the group's secrecy, both students and faculty opposed the society. But other students admired the concept of the organization and formed Sigma Phi on March 4, 1827, and Delta Phi on November 17, 1827. Kappa Alpha Society, Sigma Phi and Delta Phi formed the "Union Triad," which still exists today. Eventually, Union students founded six fraternities. This allowed the college to call itself the "mother of fraternities." Sigma Phi founded another chapter at Hamilton College (Clinton, New York). Seeking an alternative to literary societies, some Hamilton students took inspiration from the local Sigma Phi chapter and founded another Greek letter society, Alpha Delta Phi, in 1832. A year later, Alpha Delta Phi spread west and established its second chapter at Miami University (Oxford, Ohio). A member of the Miami University's literary society admired the spirit and organization of the members of Alpha Delta Phi but imagined a society of "good without the ingredient of evil." The result in 1839 was Beta Theta Pi, the first fraternity founded in the West.

The names of fraternities are made up of combinations of two or three Greek letters that usually represent a secret motto indicating the aims and purposes of the group. The different chapters of each fraternity are given distinguishing titles. The methods used in naming chapters vary with the fraternity. Sometimes they are named in the order that the letters appear in the Greek alphabet, such as Alpha, Beta, Gamma, and Delta. Other chapters receive their name from the institution in which they are situated, such as Ithaca Chapter, Lexington Chapter, and Berkeley Chapter. Several of the fraternities use the "state system" of naming the first chapter established in a state "Alpha," the second "Beta," and so on.

Phi Delta Theta, which was founded at Miami University owes its origins to a student prank. Known as the "snow rebellion," it started as a winter frolic that ended in open defiance of college authorities. The students packed enormous quantities of snow in the entrances to the college buildings, preventing the faculty from entering the classrooms for two days. Expulsion of more than twenty students followed, including

all the members of Alpha Delta Phi but one and all the members of Beta
Theta Pi but two. Both fraternities became inactive at Miami and remained so until 1852.

By the 1860s, the Masonic-inspired fraternity system had established
itself in higher education, with twenty-two of the current national fraternities having been founded. The Civil War, which placed brother
against brother in a familial and fraternal sense, resulted in the closing
of many colleges and the temporary interruption in development of new
fraternities. The only fraternity founded during the Civil War was Theta
Xi at Rensselaer Polytechnic Institute (Troy, New York). The first professional fraternity, Theta Xi later became a general college fraternity. It
was not uncommon for whole fraternity chapters in the South to enlist
as a body to defend the Confederacy. In a few cases, chapters tried to
hold together military units. Afterward, the persistence of bitter sec-
tional feeling worked to keep open the wounds that needed healing. To
promote the healing process was a task particularly suited to fraternities. Responding to this need was Alpha Tau Omega, the first fraternity
founded after the Civil War in 1865.

When the Civil War began, there were twenty-six American college
fraternities. Of these, twenty had been founded north of the Mason-
Dixon Line and six south of it. By 1861, these fraternities were reliably
reported to have established a total of 379 chapters, of which 142 had
been distributed throughout thirty-nine southern colleges. Within a few
months after the beginning of the war, many of the southern chapters
dissolved and within a year none existed, unless the nominal life main-
tained by one chapter each of Sigma Alpha Epsilon and Phi Kappa Psi
are considered active operations. After the war, the state of affairs in
the Old South was so uncertain that the reestablishment of chapters by the
northern fraternities was undertaken slowly or not at all. This tardiness
or unwillingness to reclaim old fields presented opportunities for new
fraternities to be created in answer to the need; thus, the so-called southern fraternities came into existence, many during the very throes of the
dying Confederacy and especially at institutions made prominent by
their military character. At Virginia Military Institute, Lexington, Virginia,
Alpha Tau Omega was born in 1865 and Sigma Nu in 1869.

In the late 1800s, resistance toward fraternal organizations was re-
newed. Several states adopted antifraternity legislation. Fraternities were
confronted with problems of internal administration, adequate financ-
ing, and alumni support. The organizations that lacked the leadership
control to overcome these issues soon passed out of existence; those that
survived expanded at such a rapid rate that it encouraged the formation
of new societies. By the turn of the twentieth century, the importance of
these fraternal organizations was realized. In 1901, forty college fraternities had been founded. The development of new national fraternities
has been so rapid that those founded since 1900 almost outnumber
those established during the whole of the 124 preceding years.

As one historian observes, "To be sure, the cavalcade of American
college fraternity system from its humble beginning to its present position as an indispensable part of higher education has not been without
trials and tribulations. War, depressions and legislatures have all left
their scars."

During World War I, college men enlisted in the Student Army Training
Corps. When fraternity houses were taken over by the government to be
converted into barracks, a subordinate in the War Department issued an
order prohibiting all secret assemblages, including fraternity meetings
and initiations. Had it not been for a countermanding order from Secretary
of War Newton D. Baker, a former member of Phi Gamma Delta who
recognized the detrimental effects such an edict would have on fraternities, the number of disbanded chapters might have been far greater.
When the war ended, campus fraternities flourished.

In the *Beautiful and Damned*, F. Scott Fitzgerald, the literary voice of
the Roaring Twenties' fraternities, wrote of the men who belonged to
them: "A simple healthy leisure class it was—the best of the men not un-
pleasantly undergraduate—they seemed to be on a perpetual candidates
list for some etherealized 'Porcellian' or 'Skull and Bones' extended out
indefinitely into the world."

The Great Depression forced many fraternities to disappear or merge.
World War II forced most chapters to close because either the entire fraternity was drafted or enlisted in the armed forces. Many predicted the
end of the fraternal system. When the G.I. Bill opened all colleges to vet-

erans, they flocked to campuses to either resume or begin their studies. The fraternities were the beneficiaries. The next challenge to fraternity life came in the 1960s. In the tumult of "Up with free speech," and "Down with the Establishment," many students challenged all that was traditional. Highly visible and identifiable, fraternities were considered to be part of the university system. By reexamining themselves and reaffirming basic principles and purposes, the fraternities survived with their Masonic roots intact.

Influences of Freemasonry on college fraternities are found in the rituals of "rushing" and "pledging," the rules of membership, including barring an applicant ("blackballing"), and the use of "hazing." This system of "testing" prospective members dates to the medieval masonry guild system and the oldest university in the Western world, at Bologna in the eleventh century.

"It is a system which has celebrated over 200 years of achievement," writes a historian of the system. "In its constellation are distinguished honor societies, professional organizations, and general social fraternities. In its membership are congressional leaders, actors, lawyers, doctors, teachers, etc. Throughout history mankind has devised many tests of courage, strength, and devotion."

Like the Masonic lodge, the outward symbol of the campus fraternities is the "chapter house." In the beginning, there were none. Groups were small and usually met in a student's room, in a vacant classroom or even in the woods. The prototype of the modern fraternity house was a log cabin built by the University of Michigan chapter of Chi Psi in 1846 in a woods near Ann Arbor, where meetings could be held peacefully and secretly. The first known instance of fraternity ownership of real estate came when Kappa Alpha Society purchased a lot and dwelling at Williams College in 1864. As the sizes of chapters increased, fraternities began to rent halls and houses, and a few bought them outright. Around the turn of the twentieth century, the housing movement began to spread in earnest. By 1915, approximately 600 chapters owned houses, mostly private dwellings that were adapted to their use. Today's made-to-order fraternity houses boast luxurious common rooms, libraries, recreation rooms, complete kitchens and dining rooms, as well as sleeping and studying accommodations for twenty to eighty members. Some "frat houses" have become historic landmarks, as have countless Masonic lodges.

The most famous and mysterious of all the fraternities, Skull and Bones, began at Yale in 1832. The secret group originated with William H. Russell, the future valedictorian of the class of 1833. Russell traveled to Germany to study for a year and befriended the leader of a German secret society that used a skull as its symbol. He soon became caught up in this group. After his return to Yale, he joined with Alphonso Taft, the future secretary of war, attorney general, minister to Austria, ambassador to Russia, and father of future President William Howard Taft, to form the "Brotherhood of Death." Adopting the symbols of a human skull and crossed bones that are also Masonic emblems, they limited membership and demanded oaths of secrecy.

The historian Alexandra Robbins notes in *The Legend of Skull and Bones* that it is "an elite society where the children of the rich form hidden and often snobbish cliques to establish lifelong networks of advantage." Housed in a windowless building known to outsiders as the Tomb, the headquarters is said to contain a collection of stolen skulls and other macabre objects, including Adolf Hitler's silverware. Outsiders are never permitted entry. Members are pledged to never reveal its secrets.

Writing that the Skull and Bones society is "immensely wealthy," Robbins notes that it possesses its own private island (Deer Island) and owns much property at Yale. Members include many leading corporate and financial figures, senior lawyers and justices, some ranking Federal Bureau of Investigation and Central Intelligence Agency personnel, and politicians. These "Bonesmen" are allegedly sworn to assist each other wherever possible in life, as are Freemasons. This pledge did not, however, prevent George W. Bush and fellow Bonesman John Kerry from attacking one another in the presidential election of 2004. Skull and Bones is the oldest and most prestigious of Yale's nine secret societies. The others are Scroll and Key, Book and Snake, Wolf's Head, Berzelius, Elihu, St. Elmo, Mace and Chain, and Manuscript. They serve as a recruiting ground for young men destined for careers in government, law, finance, and other influential sectors of American life. Skull and Bones is the elite of the elite among these secret societies. Only Scroll and Key claims a nearly equal influence on American affairs over the past 160 years. Unlike the Greek fraternities on most other American university campuses, Skull and Bones and its similar secret societies exist exclusively at Yale. Since its founding, Skull and Bones has inducted about 2,500 members, but the list is a who's who of the "Establishment."

The counterpart to Skull and Bones at Harvard is the Porcellian Club. It's one of a group of societies know as "final" clubs. A final club is a single-sex social club. They form the centerpiece of the Harvard social scene at their privately owned houses by allowing students to escape from the rules of the college and do as they wish. There are currently eight male final clubs, at Harvard. Two female clubs are the Bee Club and Isis Club. These are relatively new organizations. The male clubs are much older and include the Owl Club, the AD Club, the Phoenix Club, the Porcellian Club, the Fly Club, the Fox Club, the Spee Club, and the Delphic Club. They all have their own unique histories that usually involve several name changes and numerous notable members (members of the clubs range from Theodore Roosevelt to Bill Gates). Today, the clubs are most easily identified by their houses and the flags often flown from them. Each fall the clubs hold "punch season," where aspiring sophomores and juniors try to be elected as new members of the clubs. The clubs are very elite, with undergraduate memberships amounting to less than 15 percent of the undergraduate population.

In 1956, there were 3,095 active fraternity chapters on 349 college and university campuses in the United States and Canada. As of June 1, 1991, there were over 5,400 active chapters on more than 810 campuses. That's a gain of more than 74 percent in the number of chapters. Despite opposition and hard times, the fraternity system has prospered and its growth continues.

Freemason historians proudly assert their collegiate connection. One chronicler writes:

> There are many similarities indeed, and in some instances, an actual
> direct connectivity. As the creation and development of schools of

higher learning occurred, colleges sought to create groups which would provide the additional incentives of a "club" to those whose academic achievements were worthy of recognition. Students selected for membership soon realized the strong bonds of lasting friendship and fellowship that formed when those with similar motivations were able to come together for sharing of intellectual stimulation. A number of those college professors and administrators encouraging such activity were Freemasons who had already experienced the camaraderie that was achievable by those who can best work and best agree. Rituals for the induction of new members were created in order to provide an experience separate and apart from what others had known—and sometimes those rituals would show their Masonic heritage as well.

Fraternity members soon found "the companionship of like minds" so enticing that they took to eating together regularly, sharing the same boarding house environment. As schools moved to a campus environment, fraternities began acquiring large houses to provide shared living quarters for their members. Men formed groups, sometimes on the "flimsiest of commonalities, but once begun, they brought in new members and passed along the concept that being together with others by choice rather than chance was a very worthwhile experience."

Goals and objectives of many college fraternities were often quite specific, as in the case of so-called service fraternities, whose members came together to provide some type of support to the college community. Like Freemasonry, many college fraternities did not have specifically identified goals or objectives. Their sole reason for being was the friendship and fellowship of its members. They became notorious for drinking parties and engaged in excesses, including hazing rituals that now and then resulted in deaths, that were followed by crackdowns and even the banning of chapters.

Despite opposition, criticism, controversy, and difficult times, the fraternity system has prospered. "More than ever," asserts a history of fraternities, "the real value of fraternities as educational institutions supplemental to academic progress on the North American continent has become apparent."

Nearly 200 years after Alexis de Tocqueville's visit to America, at a time when Masonry was rapidly expanding in the United States, the fraternities Freemasonry inspired remain a far-reaching influence in all aspects of American society.

Chapter 17

Fun-Loving Guys

A MASONIC HISTORY NOTES THAT IN 1870, SEVERAL THOUSAND of the 900,000 residents of Manhattan were Masons and that some made it a point to lunch at the Knickerbocker Cottage, a restaurant at 426 Sixth Avenue. Noted for their good humor and wit, they often discussed the idea of a new fraternity for Masons, in which fun and fellowship would be stressed more than ritual. Two of the regulars, Dr. Walter M. Fleming and William J. Florence, an actor, took the idea seriously enough to do something about it.

The history states:

> Florence was a star. After becoming the toast of the New York stage, he toured London, Europe and Middle Eastern countries, always playing to capacity audiences. While on tour in Marseilles, France, Florence was invited to a party given by an Arabian diplomat. The entertainment was something in the nature of an elaborately staged musical comedy. At its conclusion, the guests became members of a secret society.
>
> Florence, recalling the conversations at the Knickerbocker Cottage, realized that this might well be the vehicle for the new fraternity. He made copious notes and drawings at the initial viewing and on two other occasions when he attended the ceremony, once in Algiers and again in Cairo. When he returned to New York in 1870 and showed his material to Dr. Fleming, Fleming agreed.

Born in 1838, Walter Millard Fleming earned a degree in medicine in Albany, New York, in 1862. During the Civil War, he was a surgeon with the Thirteenth New York Infantry Brigade of the National Guard. After the war, he practiced medicine in Rochester, New York, until 1868, when he moved to New York City and quickly became a leading practitioner. Devoted to "fraternalism," he became a Mason in Rochester and took some of his Scottish Rite work there. He completed his degrees in New York City and was "coroneted" a thirty-three-degree Scottish Rite mason on September 19, 1872.

Fleming took the ideas supplied by Florence and converted them into what would soon become the Ancient Arabic Order of the Nobles of the Mystic Shrine. "While there is some question about the origin of the Fraternity's name," the history of Shriners says, "it is probably more than coincidence that its initials, rearranged, spell out 'A MASON.' With the help of other Knickerbocker Cottage regulars, he drafted the ritual, designed the emblem and ritual costumes, formulated a salutation, and declared that members would wear a red fez."

Initiation rites were drafted by Fleming with the help of three brother Masons: Charles T. McClenachan, a lawyer and expert on Masonic ritual; William Sleigh Paterson, a printer, linguist, and ritualist; and Albert L. Rawson, a prominent scholar and Mason who provided much of the Arabic background. In the New York City Masonic Hall, on September 26, 1872, the first Shrine Temple in the United States was organized and named Mecca. The original thirteen Masons of the lunch group were named charter members.

At a meeting of Mecca Temple on June 6, 1876, in the New York Masonic Temple, a governing body was created and called the Imperial Grand Council of the Ancient Arabic Order of the Nobles of the Mystic Shrine for the United States of America. Fleming became the first imperial grand potentate, and the new body established rules for membership and the formation of new temples. The initiation ritual was embellished, as was the mythology about the fraternity. Soon thereafter, a publicity and recruiting campaign was initiated.

In 1878, there were 425 Shriners in 13 temples. Five of these temples were in New York, two were in Ohio, and the others were in Vermont,

Pennsylvania, Connecticut, Iowa, Michigan, and Massachusetts. The Shriners continued to grow during the 1880s. By the time of the 1888 annual session (convention) in Toronto, there were 7,210 members in 48 temples located throughout the United States and one in Canada.

While the organization was still primarily social, instances of philanthropic work became more frequent. During an 1888 yellow fever epidemic in Jacksonville, Florida, members of the new Morocco Temple and Masonic Knights Templar worked long hours to relieve the suffering populace. In May 1889, Shriners came to the aid of the Johnstown, Pennsylvania, flood victims. There were 50,000 Shriners that year, and 71 of the 79 temples were engaged in some sort of philanthropic work. By the turn of the century, the Shriners had come into their own.

At the 1900 Imperial Council session, representatives from eighty-two temples marched in a Washington, D.C., parade that was reviewed by President William McKinley. Shrine membership was well over 55,000. A quarter of a century later, the first Shrine East-West football game was played. The game has become one of the most respected of postseason collegiate bowl games. Played to raise money for Shriners hospitals and help make the public aware of the expert orthopaedic and burn care available free of charge at the Shriners hospital for children, the games have raised more than $13 million and have helped inform millions of people about the mission of Masonic philanthropy. "Players themselves regard the game in a special light," say the East-West game's organizers, "as they learn the true purpose of the game during a pre-game visit to the Shriners Hospital in San Francisco. There, they visit with patients and take to heart the game's slogan, 'Strong legs run that weak legs might walk.'"

Former president Gerald Ford, a Shriner himself, played in the 1935 Shrine East-West game. He said, "It was one of the biggest thrills of my life to play in the 1935 Shrine Game and play for Shriners Hospitals. We lost the game, but more importantly, the Shriner's Hospital Program was the beneficiary."

Dave Butz, an all-pro defensive tackle for the Washington Redskins, also played in an East-West game. He said, "The most memorable game I ever played in was the East-West Shrine Game for crippled children. I

saw kids in Shriners Hospital, maybe 18 or 19 years old, that were big
enough to play football. But they were in seat belts in wheelchairs, just
struggling to hold up a pen to write with . . . the purpose of the game was
to benefit these kids. That was worth more to me than playing in any
number of Super Bowls."

John Elway, an all-pro quarterback for the Denver Broncos, said, "I
remember it was just a great experience for me. One of my goals at
Stanford was to be a good enough player to have a chance to play in the
Shrine Game. When I got the invitation, there was no question where I
was going."

The first Shrine circus was held in Detroit in February 1906. In the
1930s, the Tripoli Shrine Circus was held in the Milwaukee Auditorium.
When the arena was built, the circus moved there. For three days in June
1937, recalled the *Detroit Free Press*, the city "belonged to a 100,000-
strong army of partying Shriners from all over the country. They con-
verged on the city in such numbers that they double-filled all available
hotel rooms, camped out in tents at Fort Wayne, filled up 100 Pullman
cars parked at the Michigan Central Depot, and made themselves at
home on the largest fleet of passenger ships ever gathered on the Detroit
River."

When the Shriners showed up at a hospital, noted the newspaper:

> Theirs is the most outlandish get-up of all Shrine apparel. They
> wear kilts, laced corset-style, and the panties that peek shyly from
> underneath are multi-colored. Their "sporans" are fancily beaded
> handbags. Their fake whiskers must be seen to be fully appreciated.
> They didn't pay any attention to the amazed looks on the faces of
> the youngsters. Fun was to be had and they got right to it. A burly
> villain who obviously had stepped right out of a story book picture,
> kept all the other madmen in order with a big curved sword. From
> ward to ward the party and squeals of happiness spread. It had to
> end sometime and the outlandish men reluctantly moved away from
> the gaiety they had created. Leaving, to move on to the many other
> hospitals left for them to visit, they looked back at the small faces
> pressed against the windows, waving and laughing. And when the

kilted nobles waved back there was no doubt that they were having
one swell convention.

On Tuesday, June 22, a four-hour march attracted half a million spectators as groups or temples were arranged in reverse order according to
which group came the greatest distance to attend the Detroit meeting.
Detroit motorcycle police and mounted police, in lines twelve abreast,
led off the parade at 9:30 in the morning. The police commissioner,
wearing a Shriner fez, stood in an open car as the city and the crowd ap-
plauded the convention. The Moslem Temple of Detroit came next in
formation and was gorgeously arrayed in green with their scimitars displayed to the cheering crowd. Next came Grand Rapids in green jackets,
gold sashes, and red pantaloons. Then the imperial potentate, Judge
Clyde I. Webster of Wayne County Circuit Court, rode in a white car
with a special Shriners' license plate, No. 1. "He stood in the tonneau
waving," said the newspaper. "More potentates, bands and platoons
with pantaloons and turbans followed. They marched to the music of
75 large bands dressed in bright satin costumes."

Through the years, other cities also found themselves witnessing an
invasion by Shriners with similar effect. Americans in other cities and
small towns were given a glimpse into the style of the Shriners in the
form of the Shrine Auditorium near Los Angeles when it was the setting
for Hollywood's Academy Awards in 1947, 1948, 1995, 1997, 1998,
and 2001. The auditorium holds 6,700 people and was the largest theater in the United States when it was built. Outside, the style of the
building is a Spanish colonial revival with domed cupolas on both ends
in shining white. Because it is the headquarters of the Al Malikah
Temple, a division of the Ancient Arabic Order of Nobles of the Mystic
Shrine, it has many Moorish details. The interior is like a tent with a
swooping ceiling. Originally built in 1906, it burned down in 1920 and
the present facility opened in 1926. It was rebuilt at a cost of $2.7 mil-
lion. It has hosted the American Music, Grammy, and Soul Train awards.

More visible to Americans from coast to coast are the Shriners hospitals for children.

According to Shriner historians, the Imperial Council session (the annual Shrine convention) in 1919 voted to establish a "Shriners Hospital for Crippled Children" to treat orthopaedic injuries, diseases, and birth defects in children. It was to be supported by a yearly $2 assessment from each Shriner. The committee named to determine the site and personnel for the hospital decided, after months of research and debate, that there should be not just one hospital but a network of hospitals throughout North America. "It was an idea that appealed to the Shriners, who like to do things in a big and colorful way," notes a historian. "When the committee brought its proposal to the 1921 Imperial Session in Des Moines, Iowa, it, too, was passed."

The first Shriners hospital opened in Shreveport, Louisiana, in 1922, and by the end of the 1920s, thirteen more were in operation. The number of orthopaedic hospitals eventually reached nineteen with the opening of Shriners Hospital in Tampa, Florida, in 1985. Today, orthopaedic Shriners hospitals serve as referral centers for complex and specialized orthopaedic treatments for children. In 1996, Shrine representatives at the Imperial Council session in New Orleans voted to change the name of their philanthropy to "Shriners Hospitals for Children" to reflect the expanding scope of care provided by Shriners hospitals. While the name changed, the mission of Shriners Hospitals for Children, to provide expert, specialized medical care to children at no cost is the same today as it was in 1922.

Shriners' records note that during the 1950s, "the hospital system's funding increased rapidly, while at the same time, the waiting lists of new patients for admission to Shriners hospitals began to decline, due to the development of the polio vaccine and new antibiotics. They found themselves able to provide additional services, and Shrine leaders began to seek other ways they could help the children of North America.

"One step they took was the collating of the medical records of Shriners hospital patients. By placing the records of each patient and treatment on computer and microfilm, valuable information was made available to all Shrine surgeons and the medical world as a whole. This process, begun in 1959, also made it easier to initiate clinical research in Shrine orthopaedic hospitals."

A Shrine history states:

Taking the concept a step farther in the early 1960s, the Shrine aggressively entered the structured research field and began earmarking funds for research projects. What began as a $12,000 investment in the mid-1960s blossomed into an international program with a 2002 research budget of approximately $25 million. Shriners Hospitals have been at the vanguard of research, significantly adding to the progress that has been made in orthopaedic and burn care. Shrine researchers were working on an array of projects, including basic and clinical research into osteogenesis imperfecta, juvenile rheumatoid arthritis, vitamin D resistant rickets, and many other crippling diseases that afflict children.

In the early 1980s, the Shrine discovered "yet another way it could help children" by opening the nation's first spinal cord injury rehabilitation centers expressly for care of children. The three spinal cord injury rehabilitation centers are located within the Shriners hospitals in Philadelphia, Chicago, and Sacramento. They serve as rehabilitation units where young people with spinal cord injuries can find not only the specialized medical care needed for rehabilitation but also "hope, inspiration and strength."

During the 1980s, an "aggressive rebuilding and renovation program" involved building new facilities, renovating, or constructing additions throughout the Shriners hospital system. By 1998, most of the hospitals had been moved into brand-new facilities and others had major renovations. Construction of a new replacement facility was underway for the burn Shriners Hospital in Boston, with a new facility to be constructed for the orthopaedic hospital in Mexico City. The aggressive building program included the construction of a totally new hospital in Tampa, Florida. It was to be the first entirely new Shriners hospital since the burn Shriners hospitals were built in the 1960s.

Another "significant decision" was made in 1989, when representatives at the 115th Imperial Council session voted to build a new hospital to provide orthopaedic, spinal cord injury, and burn care. The hospital opened in April 1997 in Sacramento, California, and was the first in the Shrine system to encompass all three major disciplines and conduct research in a single facility. The new northern California hospital served as the Shrine's primary burn center in the West, reducing the need for severely burned children to travel across the country to receive care at one of the other burn Shriners hospitals.

"Rules for all the Shriners Hospitals are simple," the Shriners state. "Any child can be admitted to a Shriners Hospital if, in the opinion of surgeons, the child can be helped, and if the child is under eighteen. From their inception, Shriners Hospitals have been open to all children without regard to race, religion or relationship to a Shriner."

Shriners international headquarters is in Tampa, Florida.

Among the distinguished Americans who are listed in the ranks of the Shriners are Buzz Aldrin, Ernest Borgnine, Ty Cobb, Gerald Ford, Clark Gable, Barry Goldwater, President Warren G. Harding, J. Edgar Hoover, Hubert Humphrey, Jack Kemp, Harold Lloyd, Douglas MacArthur, George McGovern, Senator Sam Nunn, Arnold Palmer, Roy Rogers, Will Rogers, President Franklin D. Roosevelt, Red Skelton, Dave Thomas, Senator Strom Thurmond, President Harry Truman, and Chief Justice Earl Warren

Chapter 18

The Rev. Robertson Takes On the Masons

WHILE ANTI-MASONIC FEELINGS TODAY HAVE NOT REACHED the level that cost Jacques de Molay and the last of the Knights Templar their lives during Philip the Fair's reign, or stirred a movement to resurrect the Anti-Mason Party, suspicions, fears, and open hatred of Freemasonry in the United States have steadily increased in the half-century since the end of World War II. Some speculate that important contributing factors were the long-lasting tension between the United States and the Soviet Union during the Cold War, uncertainty created by the rise of international terrorism, and the shrinking of the world because of globalism. Critics of the Craft anxiously cite Freemasonry's concept of a "New World Order" as evidence that events are being controlled by powerful and shadowy figures that throughout history have been known as possessors of "secrets." This changing group (always men) has been cited in every epoch of the history of the world, from ancient mystery cults in Greece and Rome, to the Knights Templar of the Middle Ages in Europe, to the Eighteenth-century Age of Enlightenment that spurred the American Revolution.

The name applied to men who claimed to know "secrets" was "Illuminati." Greek for "illumination," it originally meant those who had been baptized, in the belief that Christians had an enlightened understanding. In the sixteenth century, a mystical Spanish sect, the Alumbrados, or "Enlightened men," adopted the name "Illuminati." The term was subsequently taken by a secret society that sought to combat religious thinking and encourage rationalism. This new group was founded by Adam Weishaupt in 1776.

Appointed a professor at the University of Ingolstadt in Germany around 1772 and then raised to the post of professor of cannon law, Weishaupt began planning a group to challenge authoritarian Roman Catholicism. The Iluminati were suppressed in a series of edicts between 1784 and 1787, and Weishaupt was banished in 1785.

The historians Chip Berlet and Matthew N. Lyons in *Right-Wing Populism in America: Too Close for Comfort*, the British author John Robison in *Proofs of a Conspiracy against All the Religions and Governments of Europe*, and Abbé Augustin Barruel in *Memoirs Illustrating the History of Jacobinism* discuss Weishaupt's attempt to spread ideas of the Enlightenment through the "Order of the Illuminati." Weishaupt and his order, Freemasons, and other secret societies were portrayed as "bent on despotic world domination through a secret conspiracy using front groups to spread their influence." Barruel claims the conspirators "had sworn hatred to the altar and the throne, had sworn to crush the God of the Christians, and utterly to extirpate the Kings of the Earth."

Robison, a professor of natural philosophy at the University of Edinburgh in Scotland, argues that the Illuminati evolved out of Freemasonry and calls the Illuminati philosophy "cosmopolitism." He writes:

> Their first and immediate aim is to get the possession of riches, power, and influence, without industry; and, to accomplish this, they want to abolish Christianity; and then dissolute manners and universal profligacy will procure them the adherents of all the wicked, and enable them to overturn all the civil governments of Europe; after which they will think of farther conquests, and extend their operations to the other quarters of the globe, till they have reduced mankind to the state of one indistinguishable chaotic mass to atheism, from decency to dissoluteness, from loyalty to rebellion.

The major immediate political effect of allegations of an Illuminati-Freemason link in Europe was to mobilize support for national oligarchies traditionally supported by the Catholic Church hierarchy. Authoritarian governing elites believed they were under attack by reformist and revolutionary movements demanding increased political rights under secular laws. When these ideas were incorporated by leaders of the French and American revolutions, conspiracy themes became rampant. "Equality and liberty" were supposedly designed to destroy respect for property and the natural social hierarchy. The Christian church was to be destroyed and replaced with universalism and deism. Persons with a "cosmopolitan" outlook of free-thinking and internationalism were "subversive traitors out to undermine national sovereignty and promote anarchy."

Because Freemasonry was a secret society, it was considered an enemy of established order and a threat to the state and Christianity.

The heads of despotic governments in the twentieth century consistently regarded Freemasonry as a threat, including the Nazis, fascists, and Soviet Communists. The Soviet premier Nikita Khrushchev said in 1964, "Freemasonry is the greatest threat to mankind today."

As evidence of growing anti-Masonry in the United States during the Cold War, a Masonic website listed the following events:

1947

Life magazine published the article "The Age of Enlightenment" (September 5) that made "subtle derogatory statements against Freemasonry."

The August issue of the Pentecostal Evangel, published at Springfield, Missouri, had three articles against the Craft.

1948

Publication by the Benedictine Fathers of Benet Lake, Wisconsin, against Freemasonry.

Publication of Selected Messages by Ellen G. White, containing a reproduction of her 1893 pamphlet Should Christians Be Members of Secret Societies? She expressed the view of the Seventh-Day Adventists.

The *National Catholic Almanac* discussed the subject of
Freemasonry, contending that the Craft is hostile to the Roman
Catholic Church.

A revival meet held at Prosperity Baptist Church, Rocky Comfort,
Missouri, in which the Craft was berated and anti-Masonic
literature was distributed.

The Catholic Information Center of New Orleans issued a pamphlet
against Masonry.

1949

The *Lutheran Witness* (May 3) warned against joining the Order of
DeMolay.

Knights of Columbus issued the booklet *Investigate,* which had a
chapter on Freemasonry.

Emmanuel Haldeman Julius of Girard, Kansas, published *Critic and
Guide,* purporting to give the history of the Craft in its relationship "with Satan and the Popes."

A convention of Missouri Synod of the Lutheran Church met in
Milwaukee. Members were warned against lodge membership.

In March the *Observatore Romano,* the official Vatican newspaper,
announced that the papal bulls against Freemasonry were still in
force.

1951

The *Lutheran Witness* (magazine of Missouri Synod), issues of July
10 and 24, had two articles on Freemasonry by Dr. Paul M.
Bretcher, titled "To Join or Not to Join."

1952

The Disciplines of the Philadelphia yearly meeting of the Society of
Friends (Quakers) declared itself against secret societies.

The chaplain at St. Thomas Aquinas Chapel, at Veteran's
Administration Center, Kecoughtan, Virginia, issued a leaflet
attacking Freemasonry.

1953

    The New England yearly meeting of the Society of Friends opposed
        secret societies.

    The *Milwaukee Journal* reported that a Lutheran minister had made
        sensational charges against Freemasonry.

1954

    A committee of the Church of the Brethren recommended its
        members not join lodges.

    Masonry in the Light of the Bible, with an anti-Mason theme,
        by John C. Palmer published by Missouri Synod.

1956

    The *Christian Science Monitor* (February 23) published a full-page
        article on Masonry and discussed the unwarranted abuse of the
        Craft by its opponents.

1957

    Various Lutheran churches met on September 27 and it appeared
        that the question of lodge membership was the main stumbling
        block to unity.

1958

    The March 22 issue of *Awake,* the official magazine of Jehovah's
        Witnesses, had an article against Freemasonry.

    Representatives of four Lutheran groups met in Chicago in March
        to determine union and recommended that new pastors be barred
        from lodge membership.

    Publication of William J. Whalen's *Christianity and American
        Freemasonry.*

1959

    Cornerstone laid by Masons on the extension of the Capitol. The
        Roman Catholic Church and the Knights of Columbus

opposed the program and later sought to have the architect
fired.

1960

Publication by the Paulist Press of a tract by William J. Whalen,
titled *May a Catholic Be a Mason?*

1961

Associated Press dispatch from London reported that Dr. Merwyn
Stockwood, an Anglican bishop of Southward, would "censor"
Masonic services in the churches of his diocese. He erroneously
assumed that Freemasonry was a religion.

Pope John issued *Mater et Magistra,* lauding Leo XIII, the arch
enemy of Freemasonry.

Leaflet by J. E. Doherty and D. F. Miller, titled *Why Catholics Can
Not Be Freemasons,* issued by Redemptionist Fathers, Liguori,
Missouri.

The June 17 issue of *Baptist Examiner* published "Should the
Christian Hold Membership in a Lodge?" (This was reprinted
in the August 1961 issue of the *Christian Cynosure.*)

1962

The Castro government in Cuba confiscated the Masonic Temple
in Havana, arrested the Grand Lodge officers, and declared
Masonry illegal.

1963

After the assassination of President John F. Kennedy, conspiracy
theorists included Masons in their lists of those responsible.

Believers in a global conspiracy by modern Illumianti center on an in-
ternationalist organization called the Council on Foreign Relations
(CFR). The official description is that it is "an independent, national
membership organization and a nonpartisan center for scholars dedicated to producing and disseminating ideas so that individual and cor-

porate members, as well as policymakers, journalists, students, and interested citizens in the United States and other countries, can better understand the world and the foreign policy choices facing the United States and other governments."

Founded in 1921 by "businessmen, bankers, and lawyers determined to keep the United States engaged in the world," it is the most prominent think tank devoted to foreign policy in the United States. Typical of its criticism as a secret body of the modern "enlightened" is that its members are "America's elite," who hold key positions in government, the mass media, financial institutions, multinational corporations, the military, and the national security apparatus. Critics contend that since its inception, the CFR has served as an intermediary between finance, "big oil," corporate elitists, and the U.S. government. The executive branch changes hands between Republican and Democratic administrations, the critics say, but cabinet seats are always held by CFR members. Since 1940, they state, every U.S. secretary of state (except for James Byrnes) has been a member of the council or the equally suspected Trilateral Commission. From 1940 to today, they say, every secretary of war and every secretary of defense has been a CFR member, and "almost all" White House cabinet positions have been occupied by CFR members. President Bill Clinton was a member of the CFR and the Trilateral Commission, as well as another body suspected of being part of the conspiracy called the Bilderberg Group, which convenes annual secret meetings.

Among those who hold a view of a world controlled by an elite cadre, including Masons, is the evangelist Pat Robertson, the author of *The New World Order*. Published in 1991, it became a best seller and the number-one religious book in America. In 1960, Robertson founded the Christian Broadcasting Network (CBN). Being the first Christian television network established in the United States, it is one of the world's largest television ministries, producing programming that is seen in 200 nations and heard in 70 languages. Its flagship program, *The 700 Club*, with Robertson as host, is one of the longest running religious television shows and reaches an average of 1 million American viewers daily.

Also a founder of Regent University in Virginia Beach, Virginia (1977), Robertson served as its president and chancellor. Regent is a fully accredited graduate university offering degrees in business, communication and the arts, divinity, education, government, law, organizational leadership, and psychology. He also started the American Center for Law and Justice, a public interest law firm and education group that "defends the First Amendment rights of people of faith." The law focuses on "pro-family, pro-liberty, and pro-life cases nationwide."

Born on March 29, 1930, in Lexington, Virginia, Marion Gordon "Pat" Robertson graduated with honors from McCallie School (a military prep school) in Chattanooga, Tennessee, and Washington and Lee University, where he was elected to Phi Beta Kappa. In 1948, he enlisted in the U.S. Marine Corps Reserve. After graduating magna cum laude with a Bachelor of Arts degree from Washington and Lee in 1950, he served as the assistant adjutant of the First Marine Division in combat in Korea and was promoted to first lieutenant in 1952. After his return to the United States, he received a Bachelor of Legal Letters degree from Yale University Law School in 1955 and a Master of Divinity degree from New York Theological Seminary in 1959. His father, A. Willis Robertson, served for thirty-four years in the U.S. House of Representatives and Senate. Robertson's ancestry includes Benjamin Harrison, a signer of the Declaration of Independence and governor of Virginia, and two U.S. presidents, William Henry Harrison and Benjamin Harrison, the great-grandson of the signer of the Declaration of Independence.

Two days after the Islamic terrorist attacks on the World Trade Center and the Pentagon on September 11, 2001, Robertson appeared on *The 700 Club* with Reverend Jerry Falwell as his guest. Discussing the ultimate source of the tragedy, Robertson declared:

> We have allowed rampant secularism and occult, et cetera, to be broadcast on television. We have permitted somewhere in the neighborhood of 35 to 40 million unborn babies to be slaughtered in our society. We have a Court that has essentially stuck its finger in God's eye and said, "We're going to legislate you out of the schools, we're going to take your Commandments from off the courthouse steps in

various states, we're not going to let little children read the Commandments of God, we're not going to let the Bible be read—no prayer in our schools." We have insulted God at the highest levels of our government. And, then we say "why does this happen?" Well, why it's happening is that God Almighty is lifting His protection from us.

Robertson asserts in the *New World Order* that Freemasonry, the CFR, and other powerful individuals and groups are at the heart of this anti-religiosity. As a result of denunciations of Freemasonry by Robertson and others, the Masonic Information Center has noted "a dramatic increase" in the number of requests for information to respond to attacks "from anti-Masonic critics." Placing them in four categories, the center states:

"Religious intolerants" use their religious beliefs to argue that Masons and Masonry are evil. Their understanding (or misunderstanding) of beliefs is often in conflict with many mainstream religious groups.

"Conspiracy theorists" are convinced there is a huge, evil, worldwide conspiracy afoot. Many believe that the Masons are involved in this conspiracy or perhaps even leading it. (Some argue that it's only the "higher degree" Masons who are involved.)

"Hate groups" can be either a group or an individual exhibiting rage and hate toward other groups or individuals. Freemasonry is sometimes the object of their passion. "Self-servers" see the opportunity to make money, gain attention, or both. Their primary motivation is their own self-interest

This analysis contends that the religious intolerant and self-servers, "while stating an intention to obey the commandments of Jesus Christ, can be found selling a wide variety of books and tapes and asking for donations to their personal 'ministry' (usually one with special tax treatment from the government)." The self-servers "will use any argument for attention and will rail against Masonry" by using arguments of the religious intolerant or conspiracy theorists to further their personal goals. "When their 'revelations' are shown as foolishness, they feel justified in joining those who hate Freemasonry." The hate groups "will detest any other group which contains a someone who represents the object of their hate. Thus anti-Semites see Freemasonry having members of the Jewish faith and will rail against it." White supremacists "will find Masonic members who are black and thus hate all Masons." Those "not content spreading the message of love and redemption as taught by their religion will use religious arguments to complain bitterly that men of mixed religions are welcome in the fraternity, Freemasonry. Those who hate will also jump at the opportunity to find a 'conspiracy' of some sort supposedly hidden in the fantasized secrecy of Freemasonry."

Motives of anti-Masons, the center states, "are sometimes blatantly obvious as in the sale of books or the printing of postage stamps. Sometimes, though, they're far more hidden, arising, no doubt, from their paranoia of being victimized by their conception of an imagined 'new world order' or from a belief that destroying Masonry will offer them a ticket to redemption."

As this battle unfolded on the nature of elites either seeking to run the world or were in fact doing so, with Freemasonry squarely on the front line in the minds of conspiracy theorists, the novelist Dan Brown published *The Da Vinci Code*. Although fiction, is compelling story that the Knights Templars had been keepers of a secret that would have shaken the foundations of Christianity contributed powerfully to furthering centuries of suspicion and fear that within the walls of Masonic lodges something devious and possibly dangerous was and is afoot. Presenting a story of plotting among Masonic founding fathers, the film *National Treasure* made fiction seem not only plausible but also credible.

Ironically, Freemasonry in the United States today has not been as seriously affected by the controversies swirling about it as the fact that it has become a victim of modern American life. In the fast-moving electronic present, Masons find a disturbing lack of interest among young men. These youths find little appealing in participating in what appears to be something their grandfathers did to amuse themselves one night a week with some pointless rituals acted out behind locked doors, as if all the boyish nonsense of kept secrets, greetings by odd handshakes, earning degrees of standing, and going by majestic titles truly mattered.

Chapter 19

Vanishing Knights

American Freemasons admit that they face a serious problem in sustaining membership. "The future of Freemasonry," writes the New York Mason Bill Stemper, "is essentially its relationship to the younger adult male; its appeal as an institution and as a tradition to the population which will bear the responsibility of bearing it into the next century, and beyond. To consider the future of the Craft apart from the question of its appeal, or lack of appeal to the younger adult, American male, is to reduce the issue to an academical and abstract consideration—and in a functional sense, to make the Craft a reliquary of the past."

As Stemper was writing this statement at the start of the twenty-first century, annual net losses in membership neared 60,000 members, both by death and attrition. Many of the members had joined the fraternity in the two vast waves of increases in membership, between 1919 and 1929 and 1945 to 1960. By 2000, men who joined during those periods were dying or withdrawing from lodge affiliation because of a lack of interest. There was also a decrease in new lodges. Another Masonic chronicler notes that as the United States became more urban and suburban after World War II, lodges did not adapt to changes in lifestyle.

Because Freemasonry has never recruited, membership is voluntary. Previously, the appeal of Masonry to a young man was the opportunity it afforded for socializing, making friends, and engaging in what a later generation would call "networking." As the character of the United States shifted to a more "pick up and move" society and with rapid advances in technology, the young man became less likely to affiliate with all kinds of organizations.

However, Freemasonry is not the only organization experiencing this. Mainline churches, service organizations, and civic groups are also witnessing a decline in membership.

According to Dwight L. Smith, past grand master of the Grand Lodge of Indiana, fewer lodges are being created, and a vast number of lodges, especially in urban areas, are merging. This is attributed in part to a requirement of memorization of ritual to become a Freemason and ascend in degrees. Smith reasons, "Little interest is shown in younger men who, unable to spend the time required to learn lectures, degree, etc., is refused a role in lodge life. When such a young man is already committed to career, family, self-improvement, etc., he is far more likely to expend time in projects and organizations which offer him more rewards in terms of personal growth and improved skills he wants or needs to be a productive and successful citizen."

E. Arthur Haglund, past grand master of the Grand Lodge of California, observes "Change to any organization is difficult but in the case of Freemasonry, change is complicated by our history and traditions, our Masonic laws, the published codes, even our ritual, our organizational structure (Grand Lodge and Lodge) as well as the many separate, appendant groups, organized and separately led, such as the York Rite, Scottish Rite, Shrine and others too numerous to list, each of which requires Masonic membership as a prerequisite."

Membership statistics reported by the Grand Lodge of California reflect a continuing decline in total members, from over 116,000 in 1996 to less than 99,000 in 1999, and average loss per year of nearly four thousand four hundred members. Deaths averaged more than four thousand two hundred per year during this same period. Only about 8 percent of those initiated go on to the degree of Master Mason.

"We need to review the results," says Haglund, "make use of the studies and accept the facts. I submit that a real problem facing our fraternity is ourselves. We are a lodge-oriented organization yet we too often look to Grand Lodge to solve our problems; some may say the

Grand Lodge is part of the problem. Or we blame others, TV, lack of time, attitude changes in society, all of which may have an impact."

Growth of Masonic rolls has also been impeded because membership of Catholics has been forbidden by the Catholic Church for centuries; even some Protestant congregations prohibit it. These bans are based on a belief that Freemasonry is anti-Christian and does not recognize the Judaic-Christian God.

Following the formation of the grand lodges in England in 1717, Pope Clement XII forbade Catholic membership in them. The proscription has been restated by seven other popes. On November 26, 1983, the Congregation for the Doctrine of the Faith, headed by the cardinal who became Pope Benedict XIV, declared that the church's "negative position on Masonic associations" remained unaltered, "since their principles have always been regarded as irreconcilable with the Church's doctrine." The document added that Catholics enrolled in Masonic associations "are involved in serious sin and may not approach Holy Communion."

For "Catholic Culture," an Internet publication, the historian William A. Whalen writes:

> What has created a pastoral problem in some dioceses is that for a period of some years membership by the laity in Masonic Lodges seemed to be an option. From 1974 to 1981, and even beyond, an undetermined number of Catholic men joined the Lodge, and many of them retain their membership. Articles in the Catholic press [had] told readers that under certain circumstances such membership was now allowed. The general public, Catholic and non-Catholic, got the impression that the Church had softened its stand against membership.

The article "Irreconcilability between Christian Faith and Freemasonry," in the March 11, 1985, issue of the Vatican newspaper *L'Osservatore Romano*, states a Catholic "cannot cultivate relations of two types with God [Catholicism and Freemasonry] nor express his relation with the

Creator through symbolic forms of two types....On the one hand, a Catholic Christian cannot at the same time share in the full communion of Christian brotherhood and, on the other, look upon his Christian brother, from the Masonic perspective, as an 'outsider.'"

Pointing out that "Freemasonry is English in origin and overwhelmingly English-speaking in membership," Whalen finds another difficulty in Masonry:

> Both the right and the left have seen the advantages of using the Masonic organizations to further their causes. At one time, Masonry was known as a chief bulwark of republican forms of governments. Actually, in the United States today most observers would probably label the Lodges as both politically reactionary and racist....
>
> Simply stated, the predominant Blue Lodges [of the United States] refuse to initiate anyone known to be black. There is a single exception: Alpha Lodge No. 116 of Newark, New Jersey, which is recognized by the Grand Lodge of New Jersey. Stories have circulated in recent years about a black candidate in Wisconsin or some other state being initiated, but these are unverified.
>
> Blacks long ago established their own parallel organization of Masonry known as Prince Hall, along with Black counterparts of the Scottish rite, Shrine, etc. These are viewed as clandestine and irregular by white Masonry. A Prince Hall Mason cannot be admitted to a meeting of the Blue Lodges, and a Black man who evidences an interest in Masonry will be politely directed to a Prince Hall lodge.
>
> This situation is an embarrassment to many American Masons, as well as to the Grand Lodge of England, the mother Lodge, which does not practice such racial discrimination. Sooner or later, we believe, the American Lodges will have to re-examine their racist standards and bring them into alignment with the rest of society.

On the subject of Prince Hall Masonry, the *Master Mason's Handbook* states:

For 200 years, these Grand Lodges were *unrecognized* and considered *irregular*. It is only very recently that Prince Hall Masonry has started to be accepted by the mainstream.

It should be understood that the separation between Prince Hall Masonry and mainstream Masonry was not entirely one-sided. Prince Hall Masons are justifiably proud of their Masonic heritage, and there was some concern on their part that recongnition would lead to problems for their jurisdictions. However, there can be no doubt that racism played a large part in the gulf between mainstream Freemasonry and Prince Hall Freemasonry.

In 1989, the United Grand Lodge of England extended recognition to the Prince Hall Grand Lodge of Massachusetts. Connecticut and Massachusetts soon followed with recognition of their own. Since that time, many Prince Hall and mainstream Grand Lodges have extended recognition to one another. As of 2005, 32 of 51 mainstream Grand Lodges were in fraternal accord with their Prince Hall counterparts.

The Grand Lodge of California recognized the Prince Hall Grand Lodge of California and Hawaii, Inc. at its 1995 Annual Communication. We are now permitted to visit their lodges, and they are permitted to visit ours, without restriction. Dual membership is not permitted, however, because Prince Hall Masonic Code expressly prohibits their members from joining lodges outside their jurisdiction.

The Grand Lodge of California is also in fraternal accord with the Prince Hall Grand Lodge of Oregon.

Regarding charges of racism, "Indiana Freemasons on Line" asserts, "Freemasonry explicitly states the equality of men, regardless of race, creed, or color. But there are some Masons who are prejudiced, and this is unfortunate, saddening, and un-Masonic. However, it is not representative of Freemasonry as a whole, or representative of anything except a tiny minority of Masons. There are Masons of all ethnic backgrounds." Concerning the public belief that Masonry promotes elitism, the article replies:

If you mean that Masons are highly selective in their membership, then yes, Masons are elitists. But just criteria is used: men of good character, of good report, who believe in God. Does the majority of the population fit that criteria? If you think not, then you could say that Masons are elitist. The idea that Freemasonry is only open to the patrician class, the landed gentry, and wealthy is incorrect. There are Masons of all economic backgrounds. Indeed, there are Lodges which are mostly or wholly made up of blue-collar workers due to local demographics.

After the close of World War II, many such men coming home sought the stability of traditional American values and recalled that a father, grandfather, uncle, or other family member were Masons. One Masonic historian records that "They joined in droves!" As they aged and died, Masonry's numbers diminished. Younger men who came of age during the "anti-Establishment" decade of the 1960s, the "me first" 1970s, and the self-indulgent 1980s and 1990s found Masonry quaint and irrelevant. The attrition of membership and this lack of interest in enlisting in the Craft have resulted in suggestions that American lodges abandon the nonrecruitment policy and vigorously pursue potential Masons.

The article "The Building and Sustaining Templar Member," published in May 2002 by Templar Charles A. Games, chairman of the Committee on Public Relations of Duquesne Commandery No. 72, Penn Hills, Pennsylvania, urges a bold approach in recruiting Christian Masons to become Knights Templar:

We may not think of obtaining a petition for membership in terms of "selling," but that is exactly what it amounts to. It may be true that we are not in commercial business, and we are not out to make a profit, but the knack of "selling Templary" is based upon the same art of persuasion that governs everything else in the business world. We may not have a "sales department," but each one of the Sir Knights in the Grand Encampment should consider himself to be a

part of the sales force. We should be able to persuade every Christian
Mason that we are on the right track and that he belongs with us.

Games recommends telling the public

about our symbolic ancestors, the brave Crusaders of the Middle
Ages when Knighthood was in flower, as well as our modern, peaceful devotion to the same noble principles for which they fought. Let
us assure each Christian Mason of how much his enlistment under
the banner of Templary will mean in stimulating the good impulses
and the forces of righteousness in which he himself believes. Let us
tell him how much he needs us! Let us convince him by our enthusi-
asm for our cause and the sincerity of our appeal that we are most
serious when we tell him we want him to come with us now!

A list of "Ten Reasons Why You Should be a Knight Templar" reads:

1. The Commandery offers you a grand opportunity to improve
   in every walk of life through the study and work in the pro-
   gressively expanding light of pure Freemasonry.
2. It is the mightiest non-theological Christian organization in
   the world. It stands for the noblest principles in individual life
   and highest standards of good government.
3. It is founded on and draws its inspiration from the Christian
   Religion and the faithful practice of Christian Virtues.
4. As a vigorous Christian command, we wage war unceasingly
   in the defense of innocent maidens, destitute widows, helpless
   orphans, and the Christian Religion.
5. It teaches and assists you to "Let your light shine before men
   so that they may see your good works and glorify your Father
   which is in Heaven."
6. Its work presents an advanced and liberal education to all
   mankind designed to bring forth their finest character and
   works to be shared without limit with one another.

7. It gives you the richest of fraternal fellowship, peaceful freedom of mind, and a deep understanding of character enabling you to live in harmony with God and with benefit to your Country.

8. It bases all its teachings upon the fundamental truth, thereby adding greatly to your understanding of the symbolic significance of the first three degrees of Masonry.

9. In mastering the exalted lessons of Knights Templar, you learn by taking a full, active part in the beautiful work of each Order of Knighthood. Templary has no special class for the portrayal of its truths.

10. Templary extends to you the privilege of sharing its priceless heritage from the past as Defenders of the Faith and ennobles your life through participation with the Sir Knights in the work of Freemasonry's greatest Order.

Even with the Craft's shrinking membership, the United States is still the home of more Freemasons than are found anywhere else in the world. From the arrival of the first Mason in 1689 and the founding of the nation, to the taming of a continental wilderness, during the anti-Mason movement, in war and peace, through good times and bad, and despite the sensationalism of *The Da Vinci Code* and *National Treasure*, the fraternity has persisted. Its lodges and brethren, Grand Masters, Shriners, Order of DeMolay, affiliated bodies, and modern-day Knights Templars are entwined in the country's fabric. Masons have left a frequently controversial but indelible imprint on the system of government, national historic landmarks, the politics, social structure, and popular culture, and even the money and vocabulary of the freest, wealthiest, most idealistic, generous, and mightiest nation the world has ever known.

Chronology of American Freemasonry

1682	First Mason to arrive in America, John Skene, settles in New Jersey
1717	Grand Lodges of London created, considered the start of modern Freemasonry
1731	Founding of a lodge in Philadelphia
1733	Opening of Lodge of St. John, Boston
1741	First lodge in Virginia
1749	Benjamin Franklin appointed provincial grand master, Pennsylvania
1752	George Washington initiated in Fredericksburg Lodge, Virginia (November 4)
1754–1763	French and Indian War; Americans under command of British general Jeffrey Amherst learn Freemasonry and warfare tactics in British military lodges
1754	Former slave Prince Hall admitted to a military lodge in Boston
1760	Lodge of St. Andrew formed with Scottish warrant
1766	Thirty English lodges operating in "Province of America" outside Boston
1771	Dr. Joseph Warren appointed grand master for "Continent of America"
1773	Freemasons take part in the Boston Tea Party
1775	Joseph Warren killed at Battle of Bunker Hill
July 4, 1776	Publication of Declaration of Independence signed by numerous Masons
1776–1781	American Revolution
1781	Foundation of Grand Lodge of New York City
1782	The Continental Congress authorizes a "Great Seal of the United States" that will be printed on the back of

188

Chronology of American Freemasonry

the dollar (1935) and will contain symbols that will be interpreted by anti-Masons and conspiracy theorists as proof of a Masonic plan for a "New World Order"

1789	George Washington takes presidential oath on Bible of New York Grand Lodge
1791	Founding of the first Grand Lodge of Prince Hall Masonry
1793	Washington lays cornerstone of U.S. Capitol in Masonic ceremony; building of the White House begins with Masonic cornerstone ceremony
1812–1814	War of 1812; Francis Scott Key writes "The Star-Spangled Banner"; British burn the Capitol and the White House; General Andrew Jackson defeats the British at Battle of New Orleans
1818	Grand Encampment of Knights Templar established; posthumous publication of *The Origins of Freemasonry* by Thomas Paine, author of *Common Sense* and other Revolutionary War tracts
1826	Kidnapping and murder of William Morgan by Masons to keep him from publishing a book revealing Masonic secrets triggers anti-Masonry and results in creation of the Anti-Mason Party (first "third party" in U.S. history)
1836	Masons fight at Battle of the Alamo; creation of the Republic of Texas
1846–1848	Mexican War
1848	Cornerstone laid for the Washington Monument in Masonic ceremony
1849–1857	Freemasons carry out filibustering expeditions in failed attempts to liberate Cuba from Spain
1849	Pope Pius VII issues an encyclical against secret societies, renewing Catholic condemnation of Freemasonry
1859	Albert Pike revises Masonic rites and rituals, publishes *Morals and Dogmas of the Ancient and Accepted Scottish Rite of Freemasonry*

1861–1865	Civil War; lodges cease to meet; "brethren" fight "brethren"
1868	Impeachment of President Andrew Johnson involves anti-Masonry
1885	Dedication of Washington Monument; it's said to have Masonic symbolism
1898	Theodore Roosevelt becomes hero of Spanish-American War and governor of New York
1914	Organization of the National Masonic Research Society
1915	First issue of Masonic magazine *The Builder*
1917–1918	U.S. involvement of World War I exposes American troops to European Freemasonry
1918	Creation of the Masonic Service Association of the United States; beginning of the Order of DeMolay
1920	Shriners adopt a resolution to establish hospitals for children
1923	Cornerstone of the George Washington National Memorial laid (not to be confused with the Washington Monument)
1924	First issue of the magazine *The Master Mason*
1925	First Shrine East-West college football game for charity
1935	Earl Warren, future Chief Justice of the United States, becomes Grand Master of California
1941	First Masonic Service Center for members of the military opens in South Carolina; Senator Harry S Truman becomes Grand Master of Missouri
1946	Last Masonic Service Center closes in Georgia; the centers served more than 8 million men and women in uniform during the war
1950	President Truman orders renovations of the White House; workers uncover markings on walls made by Masons who built the presidential residence; Truman presents pieces of the inscribed walls to grand lodges of every state
1952	Grand Lodge of Virginia celebrates 200th anniversary of Washington's initiation

1954   Henry Wilson Coil publishes *Comprehensive View of Freemasonry*

1957   Cornerstone of Truman Memorial Library laid by Grand Lodge of Missouri; first of four volume *10,000 Famous Freemasons* by William R. Denslow published

1961   Coil's *Masonic Encyclopedia* published

1965   Masons have a pavilion at the New York World's Fair

1967   Order of Night Masons formed in the United States; first was in England (1923)

1969   The Masonic Book Club is formed in Bloomington, Indiana

1970   Herbert B. Duncan publishes biography of Frank S. Land, founder of the Order of DeMolay, titled *Hi, Dad!*

1976   Statue of "George Washington at Prayer" dedicated at Valley Forge by the Grand Lodge of Pennsylvania

1977   Publication of *Masons Who Helped Shape America* by Hanry C. Clausen

1978   Dedication of the Scottish Rite Masonic Museum and Library at Lexington, Massachusetts, on the anniversary of the Battles of Lexington and Concord

1981   Grand Lodge of Alaska formed

1982   Publication of *Holy Grail, Holy Blood,* a nonfiction book by Michael Baigent and Richard Leigh, presenting themes that would be fictionalized in Dan Brown's novel *The Da Vinci Code*

1989   Publication of *The Temple and the Lodge* by Baigent and Leigh; Grand Lodge of Hawaii formed

1991   Television evangelist Pat Robertson publishes *The New World Order,* attacks Freemasonry

1999   Publication of *The Freemasons: A History of the World's Most Powerful Secret Society* by Jasper Ridley

2003   Publication of the novel *The Da Vinci Code* stirs interest in the Knights Templar

2004   Release of the film *National Treasure* in which American
                  Freemasons use the Declaration of Independence in a
                  scheme to conceal the location of a Templar treasure
2005   American Masonry expresses concerns about declining
                  membership; publication of *Freemasons: Inside the
                  World's Oldest Secret Society* by H. Paul Jeffers

Famous American Freemasons

Presidents

George Washington
James Monroe
Andrew Jackson
James K. Polk
James Buchanan
Andrew Johnson
James A. Garfield
William McKinley
Theodore Roosevelt
William Howard Taft
Warren G. Harding
Franklin D. Roosevelt
Harry S Truman
Gerald R. Ford

Supreme Court Justices

Henry Baldwin
Hugo L. Black
John Blair Jr.
Samuel Blatchford
Harold H. Burton
James F. Byrnes
Thomas C. Catton
John H. Clarke
William Cushing
Willis van Devanter
William O. Douglas

Oliver Ellsworth
Stephen J. Field
John M. Harlan
Robert H. Jackson
Joseph E. Lamar
John (Chief Justice) Marhsall
Thurgood Marshall
Stanley Matthews
Sherman Minton
William H. Moody
Samuel Nelson
William Paterson
Mahlon Pitney
Stanley F. Reed
Wiley B. Rutledge
Potter Stewart
Noah H. Swayne
Thomas Todd
Robert Trimble
Frederick M. Vinson
Earl Warren
Levi Woodbury
William B. Woods

Known Masons Who Signed the Declaration of Independence

Benjamin Franklin
John Hancock
Joseph Hewes
William Hooper
Robert Trent Payne
Roger Sherman
Richard Stockton
George Walton

Known Masons Who Signed the Constitution

Gunning Bedford, Jr.
John Blair
Jacob Broom
Daniel Carrol
David Dearly
John Dickinson
Benjamin Franklin
Rufus King

Leaders and Celebrities

Bud Abbott—Actor/comedian, partner of Lou Costello
Edwin E Aldrin "Buzz"—Astronaut
Richard Arlen—Actor
Lewis A. Armistead—Confederate General
Louis Armstrong—Jazz musician
Neil Armstrong—Astronaut, first man to walk on the moon
General Henry "Hap" Arnold—Commander of the U.S. Army Air Force
John Jacob Astor—Merchant and financier
Stephen F. Austin—Father of Texas
Gene Autry—Actor
Frederic A. Bartholdi—Designed the Statue of Liberty
William "Count" Bassi —Orchestra leader and composer
Robert E. B. Baylor—Founder of Baylor University
Daniel Carter Beard—Founder of the Boy Scouts
Wallace Beery—Actor
Lawrence Bell—Bell Aircraft Corporation
Francis J. Bellamy—Author of Pledge of Allegiance
Irving Berlin—Song writer
James Herbert "Eubie" Blake—Composer and pianist
Gutzon and Lincoln Borglum—Father and son who carved Mount Rushmore
Ernest Borgnine—Actor

James Bowie—Pioneer, killed while defending the Alamo
Omar N. Bradley—Commanding general, U.S. Army, World War II
Thomas Bradley—Mayor of Los Angeles
Joseph Brant—Chief of the Mohawks
Foster Brooks—Comedian, famous for playing a drunkard
John Brown—Abolitionist and revolutionary
Luther Burbank—Botanist
David G. Burnett—President of the Republic of Texas
Admiral Richard E. Byrd—Explorer
Eddie Cantor—Entertainer
Christopher "Kit" Carson—Frontiersman
Walter P. Chrysler—Automobile maker
Winston Churchill—British prime minister; honorary American by
act of Congress
Roy Clark—Country Western star
William Clark—Explorer (Lewis and Clark expedition)
Samuel L. (Mark Twain) Clemens—writer
DeWitt Clinton—New York governor
Ty Cobb—Baseball player
William "Buffalo Bill" Cody—Indian fighter and Wild West Show
impressario
George M. Cohan—Composer and Broadway star
Nat King Cole—Singer
Samuel Colt—Firearms inventor
Earle Bryan Combs—Baseball Hall of Fame
Gordon Cooper—Astronaut
Davy Crockett—Frontiersman, Congressman, and hero of the Alamo
Cecil B. DeMille—Movie pioneer and director
Jack Dempsey—Heavyweight boxing champion
Thomas E. Dewey—Presidential candidate, governor of New York,
and racket-buster
Richard Dix—Actor
Robert Dole—Senator, presidential candidate, and World War II hero
General James Doolittle—Aviator, led first bombing raid on Japan
during World War II

William H. Dow—Founder of Dow Chemical Company
Edwin L. Drake—Pioneer of oil industry
W.E.B. Dubois—Educator, writer, historian, and civil rights pioneer
Edward K. "Duke" Ellington—Orchestra leader and composer
Samuel J. Ervin Jr.—Headed Watergate committee
Eberhard Faber—Head of the Eberhard Faber Pencil Company
Douglas Fairbanks—Actor
Bob Feller—Pitcher
W. C. Fields—Comedian
Benjamin Franklin—Inventor and signer of the U.S. Constitution
Robert Fulton—Inventor
Clark Gable—Actor
Richard J. Gatling—Inventor of the Gatling gun
Hoot Gibson—Country Western star
King C. Gillette—Founder of the Gillette Razor Company
John H. Glenn—Astronaut and first American to orbit the earth
Arthur Godfrey—Radio personality
Barry Goldwater—U.S. Senator and presidential candidate
Samuel Gompers—Labor leader
Harold Lincoln Gray—Creator of *Little Orphan Annie*
Virgil Grissom—Astronaut
Alex Haley—Writer
John Hancock—Signer of the Declaration of Independence
Cornelius Hedges—"Father" of Yellowstone National Park
Patrick Henry—Revolutionary War leader
Josiah Henson—Inspired the novel *Uncle Tom's Cabin*
Charles C. Hilton—Hotel chain owner
James Hoban—Architect of the White House
Richard M. Hoe—Invented the rotary press
J. Edgar Hoover—Founder and first director of the Federal Bureau
of Investigation
Bob Hope—Comedian
Rogers Hornsby—Original member of the Baseball Hall of Fame
Harry Houdini—Magician
Sam Houston—President of the Republic of Texas

Hubert Humphrey—Senator, vice president, and presidential
candidate
Jesse Jackson—Civil rights leader
Jack Johnson—Boxer
Al Jolson—Singer and star of first sound film, *The Jazz Singer*
Anson Jones—President of the Republic of Texas
John Paul Jones—Revolutionary War naval commander and
"father" of the U.S. Navy
Melvin Jones—One of the founders of Lions International
Emmett Kelly—Circus clown
Jack Kemp—Quarterback for the Buffalo Bills and Congressman
Francis Scott Key—Wrote "The Star-Spangled Banner"
Ernest J. King—U.S. Navy fleet commander during World War II
Carl Lemmle—Movie pioneer and producer
Fiorello H. La Guardia—Mayor of New York City
Mirabeau B. Lamar—President of the Republic of Texas
Frank S. Land—Founder of the Order of DeMolay
Alfred "Alf" Landon—Presidential candidate
Curtis LeMay—U.S. Air Force general, commander, and reorganizer
of the Strategic Air Command
John L. Lewis—Labor leader
Meriwether Lewis—Explorer (Lewis and Clark expedition)
Elmo Lincoln—First actor to play *Tarzan of the Apes*
Charles Lindbergh—Aviator
Robert Livingston—Co-negotiator of purchase of Louisiana
Territory
Harold C. Lloyd—Comedian and silent film actor
John Macadam—Invented blacktop pavement
General Douglas MacArthur—Commander of the U.S. Armed
Forces in the Pacific during World War II
Albert Hay Mallotte—Wrote the music for "The Lord's Prayer"
George C. Marshall—General, Army Chief of Staff during World
War II and secretary of State
James W. Marshall—Discovered gold at Sutter's Mill, California,
in 1848

Louis B. Mayer—Film producer (Metro-Goldwyn-Mayer)
Drs. William and Charles Mayo—Founded the Mayo Clinic
Fredrick Maytag—Washing machine tycoon
George McGovern—Senator and presidential candidate
George Jacob Mecherle—Founder of State Farm Insurance
Karl A. Menninger—Psychiatrist
Edgar D. Mitchell—Astronaut
Tom Mix—Actor
Dr. Robert Morris—Poet and founder of the Order of Eastern Star
Audie Murphy—Most decorated U.S. soldier of World War II and
actor
James Naismith—Inventor of basketball
Harry S. New—Postmaster general who established airmail
Sam Nunn—Senator
Ransom E. Olds—Automobile pioneer
James Otis—Revolutionary War leader famous for "Taxation with-
out representation is tyranny"
Thomas Paine—Revolutionary War propagandist and author of a
history of Freemasonry
Arnold Palmer—Golf professional
Charles Wilson Peale—Painter
Norman Vincent Peale—Minster and author of *The Power of
Positive Thinking*
Robert E. Peary—First man to reach the North Pole
James C. Penney—Merchant
John "Black Jack" Joseph Pershing—Commander of the U.S. forces
in France during World War I
Albert Pike—Freemasonry reorganizer and author of *Morals and
Dogmas of the Ancient and Accepted Scottish Rite of
Freemasonry*
Zebulon Pike—Explorer (Albert Pike's brother)
Joel R. Poinsett—U.S. minister to Mexico who introduced the
pionsettia to the United States
George Pullman—Built first sleeping car

Paul Revere—Revolutionary War hero who made the "Midnight
Ride" to warn of British attack on Concord
Michael Richards—Actor
Eddie Rickenbacker—Aviator, World War I ace, and founder of
Eastern Airlines
Matthew Ridgway—General during World War II and Korean War
Ringling Brothers—All seven brothers and their father were Masons
Sugar Ray Robinson—Boxer
Roy Rogers—Actor
Will Rogers—Humorist
Sigmund Romberg—Composer
Theodore "Ted" Roosevelt Jr.—General, son of Theodore Roosevelt,
and World War II Medal of Honor recipient
Felix Salten—Creator of *Bambi*
Harlan "Colonel" Sanders—Founder of Kentucky Fried Chicken
Abe Saperstein—Founder of Harlem Globetrotters
David Sarnoff—Founder of Radio Corporation of America (RCA)
and NBC
Antoine Joseph Sax—Invented the saxophone
Walter "Wally" Schirra—Astronaut
Winfield Scott—General during the Mexican War
Red Skelton—Comedian, and radio, television, and movie actor
John Philip Sousa—Led the U.S. Marine Band from 1880 to 1892
Tris Speaker—Baseball Hall of Fame
Thomas P. Stafford—Astronaut
Leland Stanford—Railroad tycoon who founded Stanford University
Adlai Stevenson—Presidential candidate, governor of Illinois, and
U.N. ambassador
Danny Thomas—Comedian and television and movie actor
Dave Thomas—Founder of Wendy's restaurants
Lowell Thomas—Journalist who brought Lawrence of Arabia to
public notice
Mel Tillis—Singer
Colonel William B. Travis—Commander at the Alamo

George C. Wallace—Governor of Alabama and presidential
candidate
Lewis Wallace—Civil War general and author of *Ben Hur*
John Wanamaker—Department store pioneer
Jack L. Warner—Film producer and head of Warner Brothers
Booker T. Washington—Educator and founder of the Tuskegee
Institute
Thomas Watson—Founder of International Business Machines
(IBM)
John Wayne—Actor
Paul Whiteman—Orchestra leader
John North Willys—Built the World War II jeep
Orville and Wilbur Wright—Airplane inventors
William Wyler—Film director
Andrew Young—Civil rights leader and mayor of Atlanta
Cy Young—Pitcher
Darryl F. Zanuck—Film producer
Florenz Ziegfeld—Broadway producer

Masonic FAQs

Most Masonic grand lodges maintain Web sites that answer frequently asked questions (FAQs). The following questions and answers were prepared by Bob Demott, grand historian of the Grand Lodge of Free and Accepted Masons of Tennessee.

What is Freemasonry?
A fraternity of men dedicated to the upbuilding of moral character of its members and the preservation of personal freedom.

Is Masonry a religion?
No. Every applicant must express a belief in God, but no particular religion is required.

When did it start?
Informally, many centuries ago; formally in 1717 in London, England.

Who formed the Freemasons?
One theory is that the organization was developed by the stonemasons. Another is that the Knights Templar formed the fraternity.

Who were the Knights Templar?
A group formed by the pope to protect pilgrims going to the holy land. The Templars developed into a military group and young men took great pride in becoming a knight. Many people in Europe gave huge sums of money in order that their son might be accepted as a knight. The group became wealthy and King Philip of France desired this wealth to carry on his war. In cooperation with the pope, he accused the Templars of heresy and on October 13, 1307, many Templars were arrested, tortured for confessions of heresy, and several died. The king confiscated their property as he had done with the Jews in 1306.

Did the Knights Templar before 1717 take oaths of secrecy?
Yes. Their life depended on their being faithful to their fellow Templars.

Do the Masons of today take these oaths?
Symbolically, yes. They are in remembrance of physical tortures imposed on Masons during the Middle Ages.

How do Masons teach morality?
Rituals were developed centuries ago imploring men to be faithful and charitable. These are taught by allegory and symbols.

How are these teachings enforced?
Masons who go astray are counseled by their brothers. Those who cannot be helped are expelled from the fraternity.

How are Masons charitable?
In the United States, Masons contribute over $2 million a day to charitable purposes. These funds go to the indigent for medical care, shoes, sick room equipment, scholarships, and a wide range of other help for the needy. Many hospitals are supported.

Are the Masons in other countries?
Yes. Worldwide, about 6 million.

How many Masons are there in the United States?
About 2.5 million.

How many Masons are there in Tennessee?
About 65,000.

Can a woman join the Masons?
No. But Masonry has many appendant bodies. Some are for men, some for women, some for both, some for boys, and some for girls.

Are Shriners Masons?
Yes, but not all Masons are Shriners.

Are Knights Templars Masons?
Yes, but not all Masons are Knights Templars.

Who is the head of the Masons in the United States?
No one. Each state is independent, as a grand lodge. The highest officer is the grand master.

Is there an official spokesman?
No, not for the entire fraternity. The grand master speaks for his grand lodge.

Is the grand master elected for life?
No. A new one is elected each year.

How much does it cost to join the Masons?
The average fee is $90.

How much are the annual dues?
The average is $30.

Is memory work required?
Yes. This relates to the procedure carried out when the man becomes a Mason.

Is attendance required?
No, but it is encouraged.

How long does it take for one to become a Mason?
Typically, about six months.

Can a Mason's wife attend lodge?
No, but many functions are for both.

Why are so many Masons in public office?
The ritual helps a person gain self-confidence and ease when speaking in public. Masons are forbidden from discussing politics at lodge meetings.

Is Masonry a patriotic organization?
Yes. Masons are taught to obey the laws of the country in which they reside. In the United States, the Masons have many patriotic activities. All meetings include the Pledge of Allegiance.

Do Masons become so involved that they neglect their families?
Masons are taught that they should never neglect their families or their church. Masonry comes after these obligations are fulfilled.

Do Masons have a particular kind of dress?
When in lodge meetings they wear a white apron over regular street clothes.

What does that signify?
Purity. A Mason is admonished to so live his life that no stain of dishonor show on his apron.

Do Masons perform the last rites on the remains of a departed brother?
When requested by the family to do so, Masons will recite the time-honored ritual.

Do Masons believe that by doing good works they can gain admittance to heaven?
No. The admittance into heaven falls in the realm of the spiritual, not the fraternal.

Are black people permitted to be Masons?
Yes. There are many Prince Hall lodges in the United States that are made up of only black people. A few lodges are integrated.

Are Bibles displayed in the lodge hall?
Yes. In the United States this is usually the Bible, but in other countries it is the book of the predominant religion. When a person becomes a Mason, the book of his faith is used.

Has Masonry been attacked by religious groups?
Yes. Masonry has been attacked by radio and television preachers who stir up unrest to sell their books and tapes. Other persons, non-Masons who are uninformed, have also carried on hate campaigns.

Have these attacks been answered?
In past years, Masons have ignored such talk. Recently, however, they have responded.

Are Masons permitted to solicit potential members?
No.

How do people learn about the fraternity?
Through the good works of the Masons.

How does a person gain entrance?
By asking a Mason for a petition to join.

Is admittance ensured?
No. Only after an investigation as to the character of the person is he voted on.

If accepted, what comes next?
He is asked to come for the first degree.

How does he learn his memory work?
A teacher is assigned to assist him.

What is the Scottish Rite?
A series of twenty-nine degrees, teaching by drama, the moral, and religious philosophies of Masonry.

What is the York Rite?
A system of degrees including blue lodge, royal arch, cryptic rite, and knights templar.

Is the Shrine part of Masonry?
Yes. When a person has become either a Scottish Rite Mason or a Knight Templar, he is eligible to become a Shriner.

Further Reading

Addison, C. G. *The Knights Templar.* New York: Masonic Publishing, 1874.

Ankerberg, John, and John Weldon. *The Facts of the Masonic Lodge.* Eugene, OR: Harvest House, 1958.

Baigent, Michael, and Richard Leigh. *Holy Blood, Holy Grail.* London: Jonathan Cape, 1982.

———. *The Temple and the Lodge.* London: Jonathan Cape, 1989.

Bennett, John. *Origins of Freemasonry and Knights Templar.* Reprint, Whitefish, MT: Kessinger, 1997.

Brown, Dan. *The Da Vinci Code.* New York: Doubleday, 2003.

Bullock, Steven D. *Revolutionary Brotherhood: Freemasonry and the Transformation of the American Social Order, 1730–1840.* Chapel Hill: University of North Carolina Press, 1958.

Carter, James David. *Masonry in Texas: Background, History, and Influence to 1846.* Waco, TX: Grand Lodge of Texas, 1955.

Coil, Henry Wilson. *Coil's Masonic Encyclopedia.* New York: Random House, 1995.

Gould, Robert Freke. *Military Lodges: The Apron and the Sword of Freemasonry under Arms.* 1899. Reprint, Whitefish, MT: Kessinger, 2003.

Harris, Jack. *Freemasonry: The Invisible Cult in Our Midst.* Chattanooga, TN: Global, 1987.

Haywood, H. L. *A History of Freemasonry.* 1927. Reprint, Whitefish, MT: Kessinger, 2003.

Jeffers, H. Paul. *Freemasons: Inside the World's Oldest Secret Society.* New York: Citadel Press, 2005.

Johnson, Melvin M. *Beginnings of Freemasonry in America.* 1924. Reprint, Whitefish, MT: Kessinger, 1999.

Mackey, Albert G. *An Encyclopedia of Freemasonry.* Chicago: Masonic History Company, 1966.

Macoy, Robert. *A Dictionary of Freemasonry.* New York: Gramercy, 1989.

Mann, Sheldon A. *Freemasons at Gettysburg.* Gettysburg, PA: Thomas, 1993.

Morse, Sidney. *Freemasonry in the American Revolution.* 1924. Reprint, Whitefish, MT: Kessinger, 1992.

Read, Piers Paul. *Templars: The Dramatic History of the Knights Templar, the Most Powerful Military Order of the Crusades.* New York: DaCapo, 2001.

Ridley, Jasper. *A History of the World's Most Powerful Secret Society.* New York: Arcade, 2001.

Roberts, Allen E. *House Divided: The Story of Freemasonry and the Civil War.* Fulton, MO: Ovid Bell, 1961.

Robinson, John J. *Born in Blood: The Lost Secrets of Freemasonry.* New York: M. Evans, 1989.

Tatch, J. Hugo. *Facts about George Washington As a Freemason.* 1931. Reprint, Whitefish, MT: Kessinger, 1943.

Waite, Arthur Edward. *A New Encyclopaedia of Freemasonry.* New Hyde Park, NY: University, 1970.

Index

About the Author

A broadcast journalist for more than three decades, H. Paul Jeffers has published seventy works of fiction, nonfiction, including *Freemasons: Inside the World's Oldest Secret Society* (Citadel Press, 2005), and biographies of General Billy Mitchell, Eddie Rickenbacker, Fiorello La Guardia, Theodore Roosevelt, Theodore Roosevelt Jr., President Grover Cleveland, Diamond Jim Brady, and movie actor Sal Mineo. Among his other nonfiction are *History's Greatest Conspiracies, 100 Greatest Heroes,* and histories of the Federal Bureau of Investigation and Scotland Yard, the San Francisco earthquake of 1906, the Great Depression, and Jerusalem. His fiction includes several mysteries and historical Westerns. He taught writing and journalism at New York University, the City College of New York, Syracuse University, and California State University, Long Beach. He lives in New York City.